11·28·77

FROM
Kitchen
TO Career

From Kitchen to Career is different from all other women's job books. It tells you to ignore the "start at the bottom" advice you're usually given. It says, you as an intelligent housewife, age 30 to 60, can begin your paid job life in the middle or even at the top of the career ladder. Part time or full time. And here's how you can do it!

Based on 500 housewives' experiences, it proves that, though your life may seem "ordinary" to you, it has prepared you for a wide variety of administrative, professional, and executive business positions. But to find the middle or top level job that's waiting for you, you must use your everyday experiences in new ways. This book tells how.

Each woman in *From Kitchen to Career* begins her story at the point where you probably are now. Each woman is a homemaker searching for a part-time or full-time job and career that will satisfy

(Continued on back flap)

(Continued from front flap)

her financially and psychologically. We learn exactly how she broke in, how she survived the frightening initial months, how she succeeded. Each woman's story gives you new job-hunting techniques, insights, and emotional supports to use in *quickly* translating your own "ordinary" experiences into a middle or top level job and career.

FROM
Kitchen
TO Career

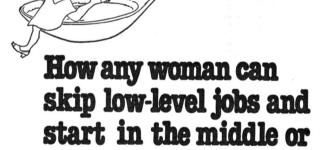

How any woman can skip low-level jobs and start in the middle or at the top

SHIRLEY SLOAN FADER

 STEIN AND DAY/*Publishers*/New York

First published in the United States of America 1977
Copyright © 1977 by Shirley Sloan Fader
All rights reserved
Printed in the United States of America
Stein and Day/*Publishers*/Scarborough House,
Briarcliff Manor, N.Y. 10510

SECOND PRINTING, 1978

Library of Congress Cataloging in Publication Data

Fader, Shirley Sloan.
    From kitchen to career.

    Bibliography: p. 254
    1. Wives—Employment—United States. 2. Vocational
guidance—United States. 3. Women—employment.   I.   Title.
HD6055.F29 1977   331.4′3′0973   77-8556
ISBN 0-8128-2350-8
ISBN 0-8128-2349-4 pbk.

With love
for my husband, Seymour J. Fader:
on life's merry-go-round,
a genuine "brass ring."

The people and events discussed
in this book are real.
Some of the names have been changed
to ensure anonymity for those
who requested it.

Acknowledgments

I am grateful to the many women who shared their thoughts, emotions, and experiences with me so that I, in turn, could share them with you, the reader.

In addition to the above, Seymour, Susan, and Steven Fader, Joyce Sloan Anderson, B. Robert Anderson, Harriet Lefkowith, Joan Howard, Dorothy Steiner, Peggy Brooks, my agent Claire M. Smith, and the book's editor, Angela Miller, contributed ideas and valuable specialized help.

Contents

Preface

During the last few years as women ceased struggling with the "Should I or shouldn't I take a job?" question and decided "Yes, but how?" they have been inundated with advice. Seminars, consciousness-raising groups, and books have offered plans for learning assertiveness, assessing interests and abilities, and mounting job campaigns.

In 1976 alone 1.6 million newly recruited American women moved into the work force. Among married women almost half work outside the home, and among all American women 48 percent are now working or actively looking for jobs. Yet even these high official figures in no way reflect the millions of women who struggle alone or who have not held a paying job recently. Consequently, the overall total of women interested in jobs is higher than the official numbers; it is unknown.

To all the above statistics, the Labor Department adds the dismal comment that unless they do something about it, most of the employment-bound women are headed toward dead-end jobs where their median earnings will be "less than three-fifths of men's."

In the evolution of the women-and-work movement, much of the formal research has depended upon interviews and surveys. In the end, the authors of these investigations have covered their theses well.

It is now time to move on to new ideas, time to recognize the splendid approaches open to women outside and beyond the already published systems. When some people hear the subtitle of this book, *How Any Woman Can Skip Low-Level Jobs and Start in the Middle or at the Top,* they say, "I don't think it can be done."

When I say, "But I've interviewed hundreds of women who have done it, and here is a whole book explaining how they went about it and how any other woman can do it," they pause. Then they declare, "Well, let me see it. That's certainly something I haven't heard of." And indeed they have not. Our successful job patterns for women have not yet been explored. They are what this book is about.

SECTION I

NO BOTTOM-RUNG, BORING JOBS FOR YOU

1
How This Book Differs
from Other Get-a-Job Books

This book offers you a new way to look at your life.

It challenges the accepted idea that a housewife has "lost" 10, 20, or 30 years from the job market and must therefore settle for a low-level, routine job. *From Kitchen to Career* is based on the belief that you, as an intelligent woman aged 30 to 60, are wasting your time and ability in an "entry-level" job. You are equipped to step immediately into a middle- or even an upper-echelon job or career.

Your years of living have prepared you for a good-paying, prestigious, interesting job. To find that job, you have to know how to think about and use your *everyday* experiences. This book tells how.

This book is for you if you have moved beyond the question, "Should I go to work?" and are now grappling with the new 1970s–1980s woman's problem, "I'd like to add a job of some kind to my life, but what can I do?" Perhaps like many other housewives, you have visited employment agencies. There you have discovered that because you lack official job experience, they see you only as a clerical worker or as a salesgirl. Even women with college degrees often meet this unyielding "can-you-type" attitude. Other housewives never subject themselves to the employment-agency rebuff. They know from friends' encounters that registering at agencies and answering want ads with resumes—"What in the world will I put in the resume?"—will prove a barren route for them. They flounder privately with the what-can-I-do question.

Since your lack of "recent applicable job experience" makes all the standard job-hunting techniques useless to you, there's only one way to escape a low-level, "nothing" job. There's only one way to obtain the middle- or upper-level job you're really suited for. You must skip the routine want-ad, employment-agency approaches and use your life experience as your entree.

But Is This Really New?

The vast majority of the creative, use-your-experience careers that new and current books suggest are craft work: Use your sewing, cooking, baking, and home decorating skills to start a catering service or other business; transfer your art interests to personalized accessories or a boutique; raise puppies for money; do customized shopping for friends; and on and on. This narrow view of creative women's work and careers does not meet the broad needs of the competent 1970s–1980s woman.

In this book the middle- and upper-echelon, use-your-everyday-experience jobs we discuss are administrative, office, professional, executive, and business jobs and careers.

A Different Kind of "How To"

We concentrate on making "how to" a phrase that really tells a story. It focuses on how exactly the women we interviewed got started. All my life I have been frustrated and perhaps you have been too. As we read a feature story about someone who has accomplished something, at the crucial career break-in point there is only a glib phrase to explain how she (he) did it. In an account of a fashion model's career we read, "At about that time she found a job modeling for a high-fashion department store where she was soon noticed . . .," or of someone else, "When her children were 7 and 11, she was hired by a public relations firm where she rose to. . . ."

That is great for Greta the Model and Madeline the Public Relations Success, but we, the readers, are no wiser after these descriptions. We still have not the faintest hint of the behind-the-scenes nitty-gritty involved in establishing oneself as a high-fashion model or public relations whiz. Nor do we have any guidelines for holding tight to such a job during the crucial neophyte weeks should we ever manage to snare one. *From Kitchen to Career* doesn't gloss over beginnings. It emphasizes them.

Each woman interviewed in this book starts at the point where you may be now. She is a housewife searching for a part-time or full-time job or career that will satisfy her monetarily and psychologically. We live with her through her search. We learn exactly how she broke into her job by using her everyday "ordinary" living experiences. We learn precisely how she managed to survive and succeed during the frightening beginning days. When you finish reading each woman's story, you will understand how you can use your everday experiences to get yourself a middle- or top-level job or career.

What This Book Is Based On

To write this book I have drawn on many layers of research and experience. I have been a suburban housewife and mother for 20 years. I have a husband, a daughter, and a son. I know firsthand all the problems of juggling family and home and job. My friends and relatives, and people I meet at the P.T.A., volunteer organizations, Little League games, religious services, and in car pools are other housewives and mothers. The things we tell each other about our search for jobs reveal patterns, if you are interested in looking for patterns and inclined to ponder them.

Because of my training and my work, I observe life in terms of sociological patterns. The career I am juggling is writing—books, magazine articles, and newspaper columns. For my articles and columns I read widely among the psychological and sociological research journals, and I interview psychologists, sociologists, and psychiatrists. I am also constantly reading in-depth business studies and interviewing business specialists: industrial psychologists and career experts. As a result of all this research, I have been asked to do consulting for companies that have been struggling to implement affirmative action programs for women employees. I have also helped run women's career forums and community service programs.

With this information and my permanent interest in people and work, I began to notice job patterns among housewives I met. Here and there a woman got herself an exciting middle- or upper-echelon job based in some way on her everyday experiences. Each woman thought of herself as "lucky" or as "an exception." Each thought her own case was unique. The more "unique" cases I heard about, the more clearly I realized we were dealing not with exceptions but with patterns—patterns that other women could consciously use to their own advantage. At that point, the idea for this book was born.

Some of the suggested patterns will lead you to part-time work, some to full-time. Incidentally, one portion of the conventional wisdom insists there are no worthwhile part-time jobs for women. Yet you'll find this book is overflowing with middle- and upper-level part-time as well as full-time jobs that women have either located or created.

To illustrate the systems involved, I collected the life experiences of approximately 500 middle-class women, aged 30 and up, from all parts of the United States, of widely differing education, Protestant, Jewish, Catholic, urban and suburban, mostly white but some black, with all manner of community volunteer and cultural interests. Every woman except three had a high school diploma. There may have been others who hadn't completed high school but they did not volunteer the information and I did not press them. Beyond the many high school graduates, some women had a year or two of college, some were college graduates, and some held master's degrees.

I did not interview 500 women face to face. It developed in this way. I interviewed 40 women in person with notebook and tape recorder usually for three to four hours. The first few hours we spoke about the woman. By then she had begun to see her own experiences in a different way. Her success was not, after all, a lucky fluke. She had unconsciously done things right according to one of the patterns. With that insight, she was ready when I asked, "Are there other women you know who did thus and so?" or when I said, "I need some more examples of women who did it according to this particular system."

Some women with many acquaintances easily supplied seven or eight women. No one produced fewer than two. Most suggested three or four. They often said, "I never thought of it that way before but, yes . . . ," or "Now that you put it that way, I know a woman who . . . ," and they then gave me detailed accounts of friends' journeys from home and everyday experiences to first-rate jobs and careers. Sometimes my original interviewee went to the phone and called a friend, and I conducted a telephone interview on the spot, filling in missing answers. Other times I was provided with phone numbers and addresses of out-of-state friends and relatives. Then I worked by phone or mail.

In this way I was ultimately able to confirm that this book illuminates a nationwide sociological phenomenon that has so far gone unnoticed.

2
Yes, But I Can't
Really Do Anything

Most women have been so intimidated by the clichéd notion that "homemakers have no marketable job experience" that they completely fail to recognize many of their accomplishments. A woman stopped me in the supermarket a few weeks ago. "Aren't you the writer who spoke at the women's forum last month?" she asked. "I enjoyed it. But there just isn't anything I can do. Yet we need the money, and besides I'm dying to get out of the house. The only thing I'm really good at is talking. I can sell the Brooklyn Bridge. But I don't want to be a salesgirl."

Because of my work, I have had this kind of conversation before, and I knew one of the key questions to ask: "Is there any kind of volunteer activity that you enjoy?"

"Oh, that," she said. "Yes. I really love my scouting. I'll hate giving it up if I ever get a job. I've been doing all kinds of Girl Scout leadership for ten years."

"You know," I told her, "every volunteer organization like Girl Scouts has staffs of paid leaders and staff people in their state offices and sometimes even in county headquarters. If you have ten years of all phases of Scout experiences behind you and can 'sell' scouting, there might be a fine paid position available for you."

There in the crowded supermarket aisle, between the detergents and the canned fish, the woman's face, even her posture, changed.

"I've dealt with the paid staff, of course," she said. "But it would never have occurred to me that I had the right experience. I'm going to apply."

Harriet Lefkowith, who directs the Women's Institute of a New Jersey community college, described to me the many homemakers trying to move into the work world who tell her, "I can't do anything. I don't do anything. I don't know anything."

When she probes, she discovers:

"Oh, the only thing I ever do is help my husband out when he goes to different conventions."

"What do you mean you help him out?"

"I just get the other wives together and arrange fashion shows and things for them for the week."

"You mean you do all the executive work of contacting everyone and setting everything up for groups for a week?"

"Yes. But that's not doing anything."

"Oh, I just run the church newspaper."

"What do you mean?"

"Well, we have five hundred families in our church. We're so big that we have a weekly paper. I go and get the ads from businesses in town so we can pay the newsletter costs, and I collect the information and put it together and then just take it to the printer."

"You mean you've made the paper financially solvent through ads and worked out business arrangements with printers. And you collect, write up, and lay out all the contents for a whole newsletter every week?"

"Yes, But two other women help me. It's not really doing anything."

"I do my housework and I help run this town committee that's interested in environment."

"You mean you're in charge of the committee?"

"Well, no one else wanted to do it. So there are three other women and I who do it. There was this factory that was burning some kind of waste products and shooting thick black smoke out eight hours a day."

"What did you do?"

"Well, we got petitions and organized a compaign and, oh, it took almost three years till we made them stop and made them pay damages. You can't believe how complicated politics is. Till you get to know how to make the town council and state people act, it's terrible."

"And now you do understand how to deal with politicians and commissions and how to get action?"

"Yes, of course. After you've been through what I have, you have to learn. But that's not real work or anything that could get me a real job."

Perhaps you believe that you haven't accomplished anything on the scale of these four women. *But that's the whole point. If women with outstanding abilities like these are blind to their knowledge and achievements, certainly other women whose activities are real but more modest may need help to evaluate, appreciate, and use what their life experience has given them.*

You may feel that still doesn't make sense. If well-educated women in their 20s and 30s who have never left the job market still have trouble defeating antiwoman business prejudices, how are "unqualified" housewives going to compete for the middle- and upper-echelon jobs? *This is precisely the key to the problem:* In the race for routine openings, homemakers lack the routine credentials. Only when they take their life experience and properly understand and use it can they emerge with unique specialized credentials reflecting their true knowledge and capabilities. Using these unique credentials, they can (1) leap up the job pyramid to interesting, remunerative positions for which they are uniquely qualified, and (2) recognize and capture great job and career opportunities that no one else perceives.

SECTION II

YOUR VOLUNTEER EXPERIENCES CAN START YOU IN THE MIDDLE OR AT THE TOP

1
Using Your Volunteer Fund-Raising
And Leadership Experiences

I Was Never a Trapped Housewife

It may be unfashionable to point it out, but millions of American women enjoy their years as full-time homemakers and mothers. Energetic, outgoing, busy with family, friends, and volunteer activities, these women meld their responsibilities and social life into a satisfying pattern. Then gradually, reluctantly, as their children need less of their attention, they realize they must add something else to their lives.

"I loved the years my children were little and I was a housewife," says Adele Lerner. Her soft, carefully modulated voice rises with controlled emotion. "Oh, I loved every minute of it." Seated in her office, one wall covered with family photographs, dressed in a quietly elegant pants and sweater outfit, Adele (or Dellē as her best friends call her) is a slim, very attractive, "feminine"-looking woman in her mid-forties.

"I was never the trapped housewife or the bored hausfrau," Gloria Brager told me. She gestured around her immaculate kitchen. "I got myself a microwave oven so I can get dinner cooked in five minutes. And I always felt the dust would wait for me till tomorrow if I had important volunteer work to do."

When I had called to arrange the interview Gloria had suggested, "Let's hold it at my house. It's much closer to you than my office is." Gloria, like Adele, is an executive, with a staff working for her. "No," Gloria continued. "It never occurred to me to ask myself what was I going to do when my children got bigger. I always had lots of friends and a lot of volunteer work. I was never bored." In her early forties—Gloria exudes vibrancy, directness, and warm humor.

She went on. "But then the children got a little older and I saw that shopping is a bore. After all, how many days can you shop? And I can't sit day after day playing cards or at a pool or bowling. That's when I started thinking about it."

Two Different Patterns of Volunteer Work: Gloria

Gloria paused as if in mild wonder. "All those years that I worked so hard at volunteer jobs, it never occurred to me that my experience might be useful some day for a paid job. Not knowing it at the time, the volunteer work gave me the on-the-job training for the executive director's job I have now.

"At the time we did it, the only thing my friends and I knew was that we were going to see to it that through our fund-raising efforts there was a religious center in this town where families could worship and get together for social activities and a school where children could get an education in their religion.

"I went through almost every job and responsibility the Women's Group had: secretary, corresponding secretary, fund-raising vice president. As fund-raisers, we were bringing in fifteen to twenty thousand dollars a year back then in 1967 and 1968, when twenty thousand dollars was a lot more than it is today. We ran dinner dances, antique shows, rummage sales, raffles, yearly calendar, trips, special events of all kinds. Then I was women's chairman for bazaar. When I left it after running it for four years, we had hit ten thousand dollars for that two-and-a-half-day event. Also, I was on the board of directors; served for five years there. I only worked for that one organization. But I did a tremendous variety of things.

"Then my children were getting bigger. My husband wouldn't let me take the nomination for president of the Women's Group. He said he wanted to see me once in a while. I began looking for something part-time just to take up some of my spare time.

"Except for office work and salesgirl work as a teenager, I had never held a job. Never. I had no real college. I went to a two-year junior college, which for me was a total waste of time. I played poker, pinochle; learned absolutely nothing. Then I got married at nineteen and had my two daughters. What was I qualified to do?"

Adele

Adele Lerner lived the full-time mother and homemaker years differently—in a way that many creative women would recognize. Adele explained, "Even though I loved raising my four children, being a housewife, and keeping a home—and I'm a really finicky, spotless housekeeper—it was never enough. I always was very involved with various organizations in very creative ways, organizing and dreaming up new projects for them to do and then carrying them out for them."

Married at 18, a mother at 19, Adele worked first for a woman's service group, started a bulletin for them, won their Woman of the Year Award, ". . . and then I left. I'd contributed all I could. I didn't want to be an officer." Then a few years as a Brownie leader. Next, six years of work for the public school's P.T.A. writing shows for them, constantly creating new projects to earn money for them, and finally the presidency of the chapter. "Then I went on to art lessons and finally joined a Little Theater; had leading roles. That was great fun. Then volunteer work with senior citizens at a hospital. By that time my children were older. My role as a mother was dwindling and I began to think I would like a job where my contributions would be recognized in the form of a salary. But what could I do?"

But What Can I Do?

Gloria wanted, in her own words, "just something to fill up a few hours, part-time, a job, not a career." Adele wanted a chance "to create, to do her own thing, part-time, to feel needed, to see her worth recognized by money." Except for the requirement of "part-time," Gloria's and Adele's goals seemed to be different. As it turned out, their problems were the same.

They were the same problems all women without formal job training and without recent job experience face. And the woman with a B.A. degree who also lacks specific job training and recent job experience faces them, too!

"When I started thinking about getting a job," says Gloria Brager, "I asked myself, 'What are you qualified to do?' and I had to answer myself, 'Nothing!' It never occurred to me to try to use my volunteer experience to build on. I thought of being a secretary. One of my children was taking steno in high school then. I told her we'll study together. I tried it. I didn't like it. All I could think of was that I guessed I'd have to go be a salesgirl."

Adele remembers, "At the point when I started thinking about a job, I didn't think there was anything I could do. I had never had any experience. I had only a year of college plus courses taken at the New School. I accomplished a lot in voluntary work, but I had no job credits behind me to walk in and say, 'Here's my list of employers or references.' At that point I thought, 'Well, there's no place for me.'

"I went to two employment agencies and filled out forms for them. It was hard to impart to them what I thought I was interested in because really I didn't know myself. I guess that's like a lot of women at this part of their lives. The people at the employment agencies let me talk and told me, 'We'll let you know.' I never heard from them.

"When I walked away, they probably thought to themselves, 'Is that woman crazy? With no training and no work experience, what kind of job does she think she can get?' "

The Job Hunt: Adele

"After that," says Adele, "I thought I'll have to start by myself." Then, reflecting the question every woman faces, Adele remembers asking herself, "But where?

"I began to think. I adore feeling useful. I've always worked with something that I felt had value to other people. So that narrowed it down. I decided it would be a good idea to work for a service organization.

"But what could I do for them? If I called them and asked them for a job, what could I say I could do for them? What could any woman in my position say she could do?

"I realized I can fund-raise. I can do special events to earn money for them as I did for the various volunteer organizations I'd belonged to. I opened the phone book to the Yellow Pages under health service organizations. The first one listed was the American Heart Association. I don't know why it wasn't the American Cancer, but it was Heart.

"I called and told the woman who was the executive director, 'I have a very large volunteer background. I've worked for all kinds of voluntary organizations. I'm very good at fund-raising. I'm fantastic at organizing and working with people. [I thought this wasn't the place for modesty.] If there's any way you can use me, I'd like a chance to come for an interview.' "

The director invited Adele to lunch but was in no way encouraging. Adele was left with the impression that there simply were no jobs available with the organization. Yet Adele persisted and made a follow-up call two weeks later. Then the director did act and arranged an interview for Adele with the fund-raising director of the state affiliate. In the interim, Adele called the Cancer Society. They were uninterested. She called United Fund (Community Chest). They interviewed her and were interested. She was told the job and salary would need the approval of the board of directors. Before she heard from them, the Heart Association's second interview succeeded, and they too were interested. By using the Yellow Pages, making a few phone calls, Adele now had two excellent job possibilities.

She accepted Heart. "It was part-time, what I really wanted, one hundred dollars a week [back in 1973, in 1973 dollars], my own hours, freedom to come and go as I pleased. Free rein to do special fund-raising events and bring money in. That's what I had told them I could do and that's what they hired me to do." This was April. Adele had till the end of the fiscal year on June 30th to prove herself. She ran a flea market and a school canister campaign. "I just got on the phone. I didn't really know where to begin. I didn't know the organization. But I wanted the job, and to keep it I knew I had to bring in money." Using the fund-raising know-how she had acquired over the years of volunteer work, Adele collected $4,000 before her deadline. Considering that during the 10 previous months the entire staff had raised only $18,000, her superiors were very satisified.

They were so pleased that they called Adele in, told her the current executive director was leaving, and asked if she'd like the job at $8,500 annually, plus an excellent raise if she did well. "I could not believe my ears. I had absolutely no paid work experience. I said, yes, I'd take it. Then I proceeded to leave there and crack up my brand-new car, which was two weeks old. It was my fault. I went through a stop sign. I just couldn't believe it about the job. It was my first and last accident."

The Job Hunt: Gloria

When her children reached school age, Gloria found that even with her volunteer work she had an overabundance of free time. While she was puzzling how to attack the job market, one of her best friends, who'd been a fellow volunteer over the years, developed multiple sclerosis (M.S.). "I used to go to her house every day, take her shopping, cook, do whatever had to be done. I went to the local hospital and had the physical therapy people teach me how to put someone in and out of a wheelchair and a car. We went all over.... This went on for about four years, three, four hours a day.

"One day my friend's husband who was volunteer chairman of the board of directors of our two-county chapter of the National Multiple Sclerosis Society was over visiting. He was telling us his problems finding an executive director. 'A director has to know how to fund-raise,' he told us. 'Without fund raising, there's no chapter. You can't spend money on patients without money. M.S. chapters send funds to national for research. National doesn't send to them. Also a director should have an understanding of the disease and ability to relate to people.'

"My husband said, 'You know, that sounds like a perfect job for Gloria.' But getting the job wasn't that simple. Our friend could only set it up for the man from national to interview me. The man from national would never have put his own reputation on the line and hired me if he didn't feel I had the qualifications to do the job.

"First he asked me about college. I told him the truth. I had those two years of junior college, which for me were worthless because I learned nothing. But once I mentioned I was on a board of directors and had had five to six years of fund raising, that's what got me the job. I know it. It's all I had to offer. My volunteer work was really executive work. Unpaid but executive work.

"Starting with my involvement with my girlfriend, I'm now so emotionally involved with my job. I feel they're getting closer and closer to a research breakthrough. I went to be part of it when it happens."

Other Kinds of Executive Jobs You Can Get by Using Your Volunteer Fund-Raising, Leadership Experience

I asked both Gloria and Adele, "What other jobs could a woman with volunteer fund-raising and leadership experience try for?"

"People-contact jobs of any kind," said Adele. "During the period that I was looking for a job, I also called an employment agency and told them I had wide and successful experience working with people and did they want me to work for them. That was different from my asking an employment agency to find me an outside, administrative job. They interviewed me and were interested, but the Heart Association offer came through and I didn't do anything about it. I do know a woman who did come out of her housewife life in her forties and did start working for an employment agency. Now she's about fifty-three and has been offered a partnership in the agency she works for, which specializes in placing people in executive traffic positions in trucking. It's a very lucrative business."

Says Adele, "Based on what I've learned since I started working, I now realize a woman with organization leadership experience—either fund-raising or plain executive work—could take over any nontechnical administrative job and direct people under her. Anywhere. Even in business."

That reminded me. "Yes," I told her, "I know of a woman who used her volunteer executive experience to obtain an administrative job at her local hospital as the person in charge of all the business aspects of the hospital's laboratory service. I know of another woman who was president of the woman's group of her church. Day in and day out she was in the church office telephoning, working with people, helping make the complicated weekly calendar of religious, social, and youth events function. Eventually it dawned on the congregation that they needed a paid executive director. Where could they find a better one than their own experienced volunteer? Fifteen years later she still holds the job. Other churches, youth centers, and temples advertise such positions. For those with applicable volunteer leadership experience in such work, they're good executive possibilities."

Other ideas: Social agencies have available all kinds of administrative—non-fund-raising positions—in day-care centers, senior citizens groups, health organizations, youth centers, and other such places. There you administer, keep track of funds, schedule, hire, supervise, and so on—all the things you were doing as a volunteer officer, only this time in a paid executive capacity.

These various social agencies also require program directors to create programs for their people. This would be true of old-age homes, senior citizens centers, resident hospitals, even jails. A woman who is effective with people and whose leadership experience is as creative as Adele's was could call just as she did. She could explain the kinds of projects she has created, what she has to offer, and ask for the chance to be interviewed and prove herself.

Says Adele, "The 'positions available' notices that come through my office for executive directors, fund-raising directors, program directors, public relations directors for Heart and for other health organizations usually say requirements are college degree or 'equivalent experience.' 'Equivalent experience' in volunteer work is what I had [and what Gloria had] and what many other women have."

Gloria developed a useful, basic rule for job hunting. "Any organization that depends on the public for its funds would be a good place for a woman with a record as a fund-raiser. She could go to the United Fund, Hospital Fund, Community Chest, Boys Club, Volunteer Ambulance Group, Red Cross, Teen Recreation Center, etc., etc. Any of them may need a fund-raising director or public relations director. If it's a small local group, they may need you only on a part-time basis, which would exactly suit many women.

"There are professional fund-raising companies," Gloria said. "These are firms which for a fee will run a campaign for a church group, for a hospital, for a community center, whatever an organization wants and needs. A lot of the people who work for my national office and for all nonprofit organizations began their careers by working for one of the professional fund-raising groups. A woman who has volunteer fund-raising experience could go there. She could find one of these professional fund-raiser organizations in a large city near her. Either look in the phone book, or ask around in your community. The professional people do a lot of work. There's bound to be a church group or organization in your town that's used them. You ask. You find out."

Adele emphasized a significant fact. "Now if I were looking for a job, I'd be in a different category. Now I could go to an employment agency looking for job placement and expect them to take me seriously and to work to help me. Now I have recent, valuable work experience. Once any other woman gets some such experience, even if it's only part-time, she puts herself into a different category. She's succeeded at a paid executive or staff job. She has recent successful experience. She's now ready for a great many jobs building on her volunteer fund-raising or volunteer leadership experiences."

2
Learning a New Job
After You Land It: Gloria

Though the job possibilities at the end of the last chapter may sound tempting and appropriate for your volunteer skills, you may hesitate to translate the suggestions into action. Suppose you do talk yourself into an administrative or executive job. How will you cope when they sit you down and say, "Go to work." How will you learn without making a fool of yourself?

Both Gloria and Adele believe that much of what you have to do in executive work is based on common sense and an ability to work with people. "I've never felt that I had any problems because I lacked college training," both women say.

Few administrative jobs that a woman could obtain would be as complex as are the positions that Gloria Brager and Adele Lerner hold as executive directors. Analyzing the ways in which both women learned their jobs and survived should illuminate the learning process you could apply to almost any executive position that you would consider applying for.

In her work, Gloria is responsible for administering the entire office and for bookkeeping of all income and disbursements in accordance with the complicated system the Internal Revenue Service requires of all health organizations. Annually she must find ways to raise all the money to support the chapter's patient care and contributions to national for research (currently $120,000 a year). She must set up, run, and direct each fund-raising project. She must work amicably and skillfully with her board of directors. She must investigate and keep ongoing relationships alive with 500 patients, offering what each needs:

physical therapy, medical care, a wheelchair, nursing care, information, advice, a comforting chat. As part of her campaigns to raise money, she must make speeches at high schools, women's clubs, business service organizations. To aid her when she began, she had one part-time secretary. Now she has the part-time secretary, a 10-hour-a-week patient-service coordinator and a group of part-time volunteers.

Adele must also administer an office and keep her books by the same complex IRS bookkeeping system. Annually, she too must find ways to raise all the money to support the division's community services and contributions to national for research. She must guide and oversee the mounting and running of the programs. Though the American Heart Association offers no direct patient care, it does provide a constant series of free community services such as courses in cardio-pulmonary re-suscitation for policemen, firemen, lay people, and ambulance drivers; heart disease risk factor screenings; and high blood pressure screenings. Adele must schedule and arrange these. She must also plan, direct, and at one time had to attend committee meetings for 13 committees as well as regional meetings. The public relations coverage that the media gives her work and campaigns also depends on her ingenuity. She has speeches to make, a board of directors to work with. When she began, she had one part-time secretary. Now she has four part-time, work-study college students, who are government-paid, a full-time secretary, a part-time program assistant, and one full-time volunteer.

Problems and Solutions: Gloria

"At the beginning I wasn't too frightened," Gloria told me. "The fund raising didn't scare me because I had done it. But I do remember thinking, 'O.K., I've got this job. Now will someone please sit down and show me what I'm supposed to do.'"

The regional field man from national spent the first four days teaching Gloria the bookkeeping system. "He talked about bookkeeping for four days. You know your brain can absorb only so much. But I learned it, and besides he left me a book that I could look it up in. (In the business world you'll find this is not an exceptional experience. The frightening procedural details of a job often are in writing for you to refer to and learn from.)

"Then they presented me with the annual budget, which at the time was twenty thousand dollars. Later it dawned on me that I didn't have a membership of five hundred people to help me, and I began to think, 'What am I going to do? How am I going to raise this money?'

"Back then there were less than one hundred M.S. patients in this area and to me that was an overwhelming number. The patients needed all kinds of help and action and information about social security, welfare, veterans' benefits, things I had no knowledge of. What could I do? I felt we needed a qualified social worker a few hours a week to handle it. To find the right social worker, *I automatically fell back on the techniques I'd used to solve problems in volunteer situations:* I talked to various people I knew who might know something about it. Through one of my board members, I learned about a marvelous woman, Mrs. Moore. She was seventy-one, retired, the former head of social services at the county hospital, with an unbelievable fund of knowledge. She comes in two half-days a week. *Now, of course, I do know about those things. I've learned from her.*"

Gloria explained something about learning the facts and the emotions of her job that many other women would find reassuring: "It's not that I came to work with all the skills I needed. I've been here seven years. I had the successes in volunteer work to tell me I could fund-raise, organize a project, work well with people, and carry out a project. Then I grew into the specific needs of this job as I went along. I learned the bookkeeping, the social service facts. I learned new emotional ways of reacting. It's hard to believe now, but I was really a quiet girl. I was always nervous in front of people. Even during my years on the board of directors when I had to get up and give a report, I was so nervous the paper shook so I could hardly read it. Now I can stand up in front of two thousand people and talk about M.S. work, and it doesn't bother me. I learned as I went along. The first time one of our patients died I was hysterical with grief for a week. But I realized I wasn't going to be able to help anyone if I didn't learn to control that; I learned."

Gloria began work in November. In January she knew she

would face a major how-am-I-going-to-learn-this-job problem. In January she was expected to begin the four- to five-month annual House-to-House Kit Campaign. The house-to-house is the collection kit into which most families tuck a dollar as it passes through their neighborhood. The funds collected are the major support of most health charities. Gloria knew nothing, absolutely nothing, about how to organize and run such a two-county drive. "I could have called regional and asked for someone to come teach me." Other women in other new jobs facing equal unknowns could also logically request guidance from superiors.

But anxious to appear as competent as possible, Gloria tried finding the answers by herself. As she thought the problem over, she realized there must be records in the office from previous years' campaigns. *With that insight, she discovered a major answer to every woman's questions about learning the job.* In addtion to direct guides such as the IRS accounting book Gloria had received, there are records of how past projects were carried out that you can use as indirect guides. They form a basis from which you can learn. Sometimes a look at the records provides a clear blueprint to guide you; sometimes, as in Gloria's case, the records provide some direction, and then you, yourself, must contribute a little imagination or ingenuity.

By searching the files, Gloria found the payroll withholding statements for the women who had done the last year's mass telephoning to locate neighborhood volunteers. She called the women, invited them to her office, and talked with them one at a time, asking if they would like to work again this year. As they talked, Gloria asked questions, listened, and gradually learned enough to figure out "how in the world you conduct a House-to-House Campaign." She asked one woman to return as head telephone operator for the new campaign. Says Gloria, "She was teaching me at the same time as she was in my office running it. I watched her, acted like a boss, and learned." The same principle of learning segments of the job either directly or indirectly from competent subordinates could be used by any woman. After all, it is commonplace practice throughout the business world for men!

As a check on what she had observed and deduced, Gloria visited the hemophilia office in town, introduced herself and asked them about the techniques of running a house-to-house.

They repeated the same format she had learned from watching the woman. So she knew it was right.

During our conversation, Gloria touched on a fear that inhibits many women from trying: the feeling that they have to do not a good job but a perfect job. "My successes these past years on my job don't mean I've gotten to be perfect or mistake proof. There are parts of my job I'm still learning. I'm still weak in the commerce and industry side of our fund raising, but I'm learning. At the same time I've accomplished things I never dreamed I could do.

"Other women who are interested in a regular business administrative job would learn also. One of my girlfriends who also did a lot of volunteer work and was president of the Women's Group was bored when her children reached school age. She found herself an office job which had a little bookkeeping. She'd never done bookkeeping. But she used her head. Bought a textbook, studied some at home, had other friends who are bookkeepers show her. Eventually, based on the bookkeeping she'd picked up at her first job, she felt qualified to apply for a job as a full-scale bookkeeper. Then they gave her an assistant. Now, four years later, she is the office supervisor with five people under her. All those years in an organization made her really skillful at working with people. It showed up when she took a paying job.

"No matter what I decide to do in the future, I could never go back to being a clerk or secretary. I've been the boss making the decisions, running things, able to come and go as I please. I like people. I like to talk to people. I like to have people around me. The responsibility in a health organization such as mine is tremendous, but so are the rewards. If you ask me, I'd say yes, it's demanding. But I love my work."

3
Learning the Job
and Handling Emotions: Adele

Emotions Many Women Would Recognize

Adele says, "In the beginning when I had first wanted to go out
and get a job, I was frightened out of my head. I had all kinds of
trepidations. I didn't know where to turn. I didn't know how to
begin. I didn't think there was anything I could do. Eventually I
knew what I wanted to do, and I thought I'd be good at it. But I
didn't think anybody would hire me on my own assumptions. I
wasn't sure there'd be any takers.

"When we were first married, my husband and I were the
typical poor newlyweds. Now he's established himself very, very
successfully. But I wanted to accomplish things and earn money
on the basis of my own worth.

"I'd taken a course about women and life patterns. It had
shown me that I had worth. That if I had raised four children to
be happy, healthy productive human beings, I could accomplish
something in a paid job. But what? That they didn't tell me.

"When I started this job as Heart Association director, I
thought I could do it. At the same time I was afraid of making an
error, afraid of stumbling and making a fool of myself. I was
confident in the kind of work I was doing because I knew from all
those years of volunteer projects that I did my best in these kinds
of situations. Yet it was a mixture of confidence and optimism and
the natural fears of being in a totally new, demanding job.

Two weeks after they had offered Adele the Heart Association
directorship (and she had crashed her car in the excitement), the

current director left. Adele recalls, "I had to start from scratch. She hadn't shown me a thing. Maybe she resented someone as green as me taking over the job. Luckily the secretary had been there two years. She knew the mechanics well enough to help me in areas that I knew nothing about [again, learning from a subordinate, as Gloria did]. I had to take over every aspect of the office, administration, community services, committee meetings, fund raising. When I started two years ago, we were raising twenty-two thousand dollars. Last year it was seventy-three thousand dollars, and our goal next year is one hundred thousand dollars.

"I learned and I'm still learning. It was all trial and error. The first year I worked a twelve-hour day because I took work home. I wanted so much for it to succeed. I enjoy it. It was a labor of love. I think that's the most important thing for any woman: that she find something she likes to do. The first months I was groping along. I can't remember what I'd done, but I do recall not sleeping some nights worrying about a mistake I'd made.

"One of the important things I learned that other women might also have to adjust to is not being too sensitive or taking things too personally. One of the directors I work with never pointed his criticism at a situation, always at me. I used to get uptight, even when he was only teasing. He'd say to me on the phone, 'Well, did you make fifty thousand dollars this month?' I'd hang up the phone and say, 'What does he mean? He knows I can't raise fifty thousand dollars in one month.' Now I realize that's just his way of talking. And different people will have different ways.

"The very first week after I took on the job, I had a board meeting to prepare for. I had to make up the agenda, prepare committee reports, everything. It was a tremendous challenge to face so soon. But I did it. I looked at how past meeting agendas and reports were organized (as Gloria checked past house-to-house procedure), and I came through. Then, in the following months, I took each aspect of the Heart Association and worked with it separately to make it functional, viable."

Adele's system for developing each aspect of the organization was the same checking-what-was-done-in-the-past that any woman can use for any job. As she learned and gained experience, Adele added, changed, and developed her own approaches. Soon she was innovating numerous programs that had never been attempted before. The same would be true for other women: Once you understand the framework of the job, your years of creative organizational experience can surface and begin contributing to your current assignments

Beginning with the past is not only practical, but is also excellent industrial and management psychology. As Dr. Joel Moses, Director of Personnel Research for A.T.&T. and an editor of *Personnel Psychology* commented when I interviewed him on the question, the executive who comes in and immediately sets up new routines and new systems is a threatening figure. She/he may arouse instant wildfire antagonisms as the subordinates begin to fear a general changeover that may affect their own jobs. Far better to begin with old routines and change gradually as the executive and subordinates get to know one another.

Assets

"The knowledge and all the contacts I made during my years of volunteer work have been invaluable. Knowing where to go, whom to contact, what to do, where to reach out to accomplish certain things has made it much easier for me to succeed at an administrative job like mine." How well Adele has learned her job was dramatized by a recent on-site inspection of her chapter's activities by her state superiors. Their report was glowing; the summary word they used was "superior."

Every community has a personality, special features that only someone with experience working in that community understands. Long-time residence is an aid. A few years of active community volunteer work are an excellent substitute. These years equip a woman with a network of facts, insights, and acquaintances that will aid her in any executive work she obtains in that locality.

Growth as a Person

As Adele sees it, "During the two years I've worked, I've not only grown in the job, but it's been like a new me evolving with my children too. I was always a devoted mother. I still am. I never let my children do a lot of things, go a lot of places. I was very cautious of them. Now the new me would have been less cautious, would have limited my children less. I used to keep my youngest daughter out of school for the slightest illness to give me companionship. I think a lot of women do that. I think my working has benefited my children. Though, of course, there's only one at home full-time since I've been working.

"I've always been a very happy person, and working just added to it. The Association is something I've built. I want to nurture it, do what I can. And I've met such fantastic people on the job: the board, the doctors, the nurses, the volunteers. People I would otherwise never have met. If I had remained at home, I would have been unhappy by now. It was certainly no longer enough."

4

Maybe You Are Already Sitting Atop a Great Potential Career

I bicycled to a friend's house last Saturday. When I arrived, I discovered she already had a visitor, Paula Blauvelt, a former neighbor who had dropped in to renew their acquaintance. While we talked, Paula's two-year-old napped, and her five- and ten-year-old played on the grass outside. At one point Paula sighed. "I was so embarrassed last week," she said. "I got a letter from a college friend of mine. She's gone back and taken her master's in business, and she has a fantastic job as an executive with a utility company. When I sat down to write to her, I drew a blank. For thirteen years I haven't done a thing."

"You've created three human beings," I protested. "You just finished telling us about the volunteer activities you help run at your church." She barely noticed my comment. Still lost in her dissatisfaction with herself, she repeated, "I had nothing to write. I haven't done anything for thirteen years."

This section is for everyone who, even fleetingly, has felt as Paula Blauvelt does. As long as you think that way, you will see yourself and present yourself to others as someone "who hasn't done anything," and you will be helpless. Once you begin to look realistically at how you have been occupying yourself during the last thirteen, seventeen, twenty-five years, you have the qualifications, self-esteem and ability to land or create a great job or career for yourself.

It is a rare woman who has not done some (not a tremendous amount, just some) volunteer work for a community, cultural, philanthropic, environmental, political, religious, youth, or educational cause. The skills you developed planning and carrying out these volunteer tasks can point you toward a great paid part-time or full-time career whenever you are ready.

Hidden Abilities That Can Earn You Money

First, realize that the *volunteer responsibilities* you have accepted and enjoyed over the years probably suggest your hidden paid-work abilities. If you accept the task of youth volunteer leader and find the duties difficult and uncongenial, will you take that assignment again? Of course not. You will move on, trying other responsibilities until you discover an activity you enjoy. Therefore, the volunteer responsibilities you have accepted *over a period of time* represent what you do easily and well and what interests you—or you would not be doing them! Stop and list the volunteer assignments you have enjoyed as the first step toward defining a paid career that will suit and excite you.

For example, do you find it easy as chairperson to keep your committee working enthusiastically? Most people do not. You may have two precious talents on which you could build your paid work life: ability to work with people and organizational skill. Does arranging for publicity for your group or preparing its newsletter seem a fun and easy assignment? Most people find it overwhelming. You probably have the aptitudes to be happy working in some aspect of communications or public relations. Do you usually gravitate to youth group leadership? Most women regard volunteer work as time off from their own children. They would never take on the offspring of strangers. Your liking for the activity probably indicates empathy and ability that would make you a successful paid youth leader or social worker.

Don't Move: Maybe You Are Already Sitting Atop a Potential Career

Now that you have begun discovering what you enjoy doing, there may be a paid job or career waiting for you in your present volunteer organization. In the second chapter I mentioned the woman with ten years of Girl Scout volunteer work. Just as that woman applied for and obtained an exciting part-time job with her state's professional Girl Scout staff, you may be able to do the same with your volunteer group's paid staff.

Simpler yet and very common is the situation where you develop your job directly from your volunteer activity itself. For example, four young mothers in suburban San Diego spent months as volunteers researching, ordering books for, setting up, and cataloguing an entire public school library. The school principal eventually asked if they were interested in becoming the school's librarians. Two of the women were interested. They accepted the job and while they worked took the necessary courses during summers and evenings. Another woman I interviewed, Alice Beinbach, did volunteer work with cerebral palsy children at the county center. She began with a few hours a week and was drawn into the work. By year's end she was occupied two to three days weekly with it, and she asked the director if additional teachers were needed. By then the director recognized Alice's ability with the children and offered her a three-day-a-week paid position. Alice enrolled for specialized teaching courses to qualify for the title and good pay, but she possessed the job while studying.

The same pattern exists in the arts. Susan Stewart began as a singer in 1966 with an established semiprofessional singing group, the Pro Arte Chorale. Everyone in the group except the director is a volunteer. As the years passed, Susan joined the group's board of trustees. Then she volunteered to keep a scrapbook of the group's concert reviews, publicity, travels. This led very soon to doing publicity. Handling this job, Susan found, meant muddling through the chorale's confused office records in order to obtain facts she needed. "I volunteered to come into the office and try to straighten out the records and files. Oh my, how I worked. We'd never had any paid staff, and things were every which way." Several months after she began spending days at the chorale office, the group received a state grant for a cultural project that required a part-time office manager. Who, logically, in all the chorale was best suited for that paid position? Susan Stewart, of course. Wasn't she already a volunteer there at the office, knowledgeable, interested, and experienced?

Part-Time? Full-Time? You May Change Your Mind

Lee Porter's growth from part-time volunteer to part-time paid worker to full-time paid worker is typical of many, many women's experiences. Though almost every woman fervently searches for part-time work when making the transition from full-time homemaker, many soon discover they want their career to expand to full-time. What was once "too much" becomes practical and attractive a few years later when the children are older and have moved to greater self-reliance. Lee, a black woman married to a mechanical engineer, volunteered to work at her county Fair Housing Council after the Council had aided her family. "I saw more houses for sale in one day with the Council's help than real estate agents had been willing to show us during the previous four months." For seven years Lee contributed time and effort as a volunteer with the agency. Her daughters were 12 and 6 when she began, and six years later her son was born. "The Council's basic purpose is to put itself out of business by breaking down prejudices until houses and apartments will not be rented or sold on the basis of color or creed," says Lee.

When funding made it possible for Fair Housing to hire a staff, a minister became the first executive director, and Lee and other volunteers became part-time paid workers. With a preschooler at home, that was all Lee could manage. Two years later when the minister retired, Lee was offered the executive directorship; her hours would be from nine to three, plus evening and weekend meetings, and she would have to make speeches to community and religious organizations throughout the county. Lee, a slim and very pretty woman, smiled as she recalled, "By then my son was in school all day, and what had been impossible was now practical. My oldest daughter was seventeen and well able to help, as, of course, my husband does."

Lee has been executive director for five years. She supervises an organization with forty-six hundred members, an in-office staff of associate director, housing director, lawyer, legal assistant, legal secretary, receptionist, 6 to 10 part-time volunteer clerical workers, and 60 to 100 part-time volunteer "family escorts" and "testers" who work with an annual caseload of about 300 to 500 families. "We've been effective; sixty-nine of the county's seventy towns now have at least a few black families living in them."

Both the associate director and housing director, whose positions are part-time, were also long-time volunteers. Says Lee, "Like me they were housewives working voluntarily for a cause they believed in. We all had to be convinced to work for pay when we were funded. But the various government and United Fund officers who provided the financial support pointed out to us that it was wasteful of the limited funding money to hire brand-new people who had to be trained. They insisted that those of us who had been working all these years were the best qualified to do the job."

Three Ways to Think Out Your Own Solution   2010923

1. What career do you suspect you might enjoy? Just as the San Diego women tested their interest in library work by volunteering to create the school library, you can test your reactions to an occupation by volunteering. Two of the four women discovered that though they enjoyed developing the library as a one-time experience, it did not appeal to them as a permanent occupation. The other two women did find their career answers through this volunteer effort. When they were offered library positions, they were sure of their pleasure in the profession and enrolled for the necessary courses, backed by jobs already secured.

If you follow this route, ascertain which courses the college will allow you credit for based on your life and volunteer experiences. Shop around among the colleges in your area. Each has different rulings. But it is almost universal practice nowadays for colleges to grant adults *some* credits through the College Level Equivalency Program (C.L.E.P.) examinations and through personal interviews. Besides obvious credit-garnering experiences such as setting up the library, you can receive credit for many volunteer activities. One woman who had been chairperson of a town P.T.A. committee was excused from a two-unit business communications course when she submitted copies of letters she had written as PTA chairlady arranging for speakers and various civic projects. Another woman received political science credit for work she had done in local political campaigns. Your college office can supply details, but it is up to you to look through the courses you are supposed to take, while asking yourself, "What did I do as a volunteer that could meet this requirement?" The basic joyful point is this: Wherever you qualify under these programs, you are excused from taking those courses but are nevertheless awarded college credits for them toward a degree.

2. When Alice Beinbach, the cerebral palsy volunteer, discovered her satisfaction with the work, she asked the director for a position. Sounds simple, doesn't it?

Yet there is no way of adding up all the job heartaches and career disappointments women endure becaue they fail to take this simple step. As interest in careers for women has grown, analysts and employment experts have noticed a women's outlook that might be dubbed the if-I'm-efficient-I'll-be-noticed-and-rewarded attitude. Probably because of social conditioning, women fail to ask for pay increases, fail to make clear to their superiors that they are interested in promotion, fail to indicate they are willing to assume more responsibility. Instead they toil meticulously and wait passively to be noticed.

Sometimes, as with the principal who offered the women the jobs as librarians, competence is noticed and rewarded. More often the busy superiors, who have their own careers, problems, and responsibilities on their minds, never react. As they see it, yes, you are doing a good job. But since you never mention wanting a paid job, or other assignments, or promotions, or more money, apparently you are satisfied. When they do need a new employee or someone for a promotion, they "just don't think of" suggesting it to the silent, competent hopeful right there in their own domain—unless that hopeful has pleasantly put the idea into the superior's head by making clear her aspirations.

3. Are you, like Susan Stewart or Lee Porter, a volunteer for a community or cultural organization? A pattern exists in these groups that you can use. Usually begun as 100 percent volunteer efforts, these organizations—if they prosper—eventually require paid executive staff. Almost always these staff administrative

positions begin as part-time assignments, as Lee Porter's was and Susan Stewart's still is. As such they are truly dream jobs from the homemaker's viewpoint—exciting, important, interesting, and part-time besides! The experience of Mary F. Holloway in New York City can be echoed in communities across the country. Long active in various community organizations, her experience has carried her to the salaried part-time office of executive director of Volunteers to Improve Third Avenue and Lexington (V.I.T.A.L.). You gain a glimpse of the excitement and scope of her work life when you learn that V.I.T.A.L. consists of 70 businesses and citizens' groups.

You can speed your group's ability to hire and pay for a director by making an effort to obtain a grant from a government agency or private foundation. It is often easier than it might sound.

Private foundations annually spend more than two billion dollars in grants. No one seems to know the multi-billion-dollar size of government grants. When I inquired, the Foundation Center, with national "foundation libraries" in New York and Washington and regional collections throughout the nation, recoiled in distress at the thought of trying to produce a total. A United States senator's aide who specializes in helping constituents prepare and present grant proposals to government was equally nonplussed at the thought of compiling an overall total. To give you an idea, though, of the potential waiting there for you, one federal agency alone—Health, Eduation, and Welfare (HEW)—in one year gave six billion dollars to higher education projects and another four billion dollars to health and social welfare community groups. Billions more go to community, cultural, civic, environmental, and other projects of all kinds. Notice those are billions, not millions. State governments hand out additional dollars in state-financed grants or federally financed grants that are channeled through state offices. Some groups in your community are taking in that money. *Why not yours?*

The Foundation Directory, published by the Foundation Center and distributed by Columbia University Press, is available in many public libraries. It lists some 26,000 private American Foundations (giants such as Ford and Rockefeller and thousands of small ones), their addresses, their areas of interests, and the types of grants they offer. The key phrase in the last sentence is "areas of interest." Some foundations are interested in underprivileged children, some in mental health, some in community housing, some in innovative educational ideas, some in art, some in civil rights, and so on. Because foundations focus their interests, your task is much simpler. You can quickly narrow it to ones that support projects such as yours. To aid you, the Foundation Center (888 Seventh Avenue, New York, New York 10019) will send you without charge addresses of foundation libraries near you as well as useful leaflets such as *What Will a Foundation Look for When You Submit a Grant Proposal?* by Robert A. Mayer and *What Makes a Good Proposal?* by F. Lee Jacquette and Barbara I. Jacquette.

In his leaflet Mayer makes some very encouraging observations. "Small, often family-operated foundations can be a good source of support for a project whose impact will be localized. . . . See if you can put together a combination of financial aid from the smaller foundations. These organizations are often staffed by individuals who are doing the work as a second job . . . they may be attorneys for the family who supports the foundation. Therefore they have neither the time nor the experience to permit deep analysis of proposals. An exciting project, soundly conceived and presented in a well-documented manner can make a strong showing here. It makes the part-time foundation manager's job easier."

Two books that you may be able to obtain from your library have been commended by the Foundation Center as containing useful material: *The Art of Winning Foundation Grants* by Howard Hillman and Karen Arabanel (New York: Vanguard Press, 1975) and *Grants: How to Find Out About Them and What to Do Next* by Virginia White (New York: Plenum Press, 1975). The first book deals only with private foundations; the second discusses both private and government funding. To obtain your share of that lode of government grants, you may best begin by contacting your United States senators' or your United States congressperson's offices. For state grant information, contact your state legislator's office; the people there can do much to help you avoid the bureaucratic labyrinth.

Contact your congresspeople and state legislator. Explain your organization's activities and purpose, and *mention how many members you have from their voting districts.* They will instantly translate that membership into votes. Ask them to obtain information for you about federal and state government funding and grants that are available for organizations such as yours. *You are not asking for influence, only for information.* With all those votes possibly riding on the response, you can be sure that some bright assistant will be assigned to dig for the pertinent facts and report them to you. They will then—if you ask them to—often help you develop and present your proposal.

Some legislators place so great an emphasis on helping constituents obtain the grants their projects deserve that they permanently assign aides to develop constituents' proposals. These experts will put considerable official energy into creating and steering your proposals through governmental red tape to a successful conclusion. Even when legislators have no designated grant specialist, your group will still represent votes to them, so they will put someone competent on the job for you.

What can a small group or even one interested person hope to accomplish when applying to a legislator for grant aid?

N.A.R.C.O., a drug rehabilitation program in Atlantic City, New Jersey, has been so successful it has become a national model. It began when an ex-drug user, John Brooks, walked into the office of New Jersey's U.S. Senator Harrison Williams and asked for assistance in obtaining funding to develop the project. An aide who specializes in grants spoke with Brooks, helped him collect a suitable citizens' committee, and then worked with the group to write the grant proposal and see it through to success. The result was 8.2 million dollars in funding over six years and, of course, Brooks as executive director.

To give you an idea of the range of government funding: Other recent groups successfully funded by Senator Williams's constituents include the Garden State Ballet, the Newark Boys Choir, and the world-famous Victorian curiosity, Lucy, the Margate City seaside elephant—a building shaped like an elephant—all of which received grants from the National Endowment for the Humanities. The money for architectural and structural work to keep "Lucy" from collapsing was obtained by a group of local citizens banded together into the "Save Lucy Committee." Senator Williams's grant specialist, Wallace Johnson, reports, 'We have about eight hundred grant proposals that we're working on at any given time. We try to work through our project load every eight months. If there is a genuine need for the project, we can often accomplish a lot."

Since it is the job of legislators to represent the interests of their districts, they are usually extremely happy to act as intermediaries and thus gain your group's goodwill. When the money comes through, you are the person who has led the funding effort and therefore the one who knows the most about the project, the one best suited to administer it as the part-time or full-time paid organizational staff director.

5
Other Practical Ways to Turn Volunteer Work into a High-Level Paid Job

Take your premarriage occupation, and add your volunteer work. Then what do you have?

You have a brand-new mix of talent, training, and experience. For Karen Ostrow, a dark-haired woman with pixie charm, it has meant admission to the world of theater. Karen recalls that as a child and later as an elementary school teacher, she had not the faintest idea she had dramatic or writing talent. Yet today she has four part-time, well-paying jobs writing and directing children's plays for her town, the Y, and two Sunday schools. She is half of the writing team of a quality professional drama group for young people's plays. From that drama group she and some other members have spun off into writing a U.H.F. T.V. play, advertising jingles, and plots for advertising skits. "It's a very exciting business," says Karen. "You never know what's around the corner, what today's activity can lead to tomorrow." Karen's posture and the exhilaration in her face testified to how wonderful it was to have invented in mid-life a career that promised open-ended possibilities.

"With three children and a husband, I absolutely could not handle a full-time job. So all I did was occasional elementary school substituting. Then a woman's group I belonged to asked me to write and direct a play about the group's activities. Just a little entertainment for one of our monthly meetings.

"You have to realize that when I first married, I was so unsure of myself I wouldn't take the chairmanship for anything. I'd joined the women's group to meet people in our new suburban town and that was it. Eventually I accepted a tiny responsibility and saw it wasn't so terrible, then more and more."

Karen invited a friend, Celia, to write the women's group play with her. They chose a musical comedy format: using popular tunes, creating their own lyrics and story. "Celia didn't know she could write," Karen said. "But we clicked immediately. The minute I wrote the first lyrics I realized I could do it with ease and pleasure. And Celia has talent, we discovered, for plays."

Karen's and Celia's production was so successful that word of mouth soon brought them requests to write a segment of the P.T.A. annual scholarship show; then their hometown asked them to create a musical comedy about the town for summer bandshell presentation. "If anyone has *any ability* and is giving it away free on a volunteer basis as we were, *they'll have a chance to build and develop that talent.* There are always organizations who will hear about you and give you a chance to work," says Karen. "Besides you can tell people you're available."

It was the director of the town bandshell show—a housewife who had never before used her college drama training—who suggested incorporating the bandshell cast into a professional children's troupe. So the Tel-A-Story players were born. There are 11 members. By going out and drumming up engagements, they have played shopping centers, organizations, schools, and Off-Broadway in New York. "Now we have people pounding on our door trying to get into the company. We can't use anyone else." (Karen explains that by "drumming up engagements" they mean they wrote to program chairpeople of organizations, enclosing play flyers and photocopies of good reviews they had received. They did the same with public relations directors at shopping centers and school principals; the Off-Broadway show-ing they achieved by renting the theater themselves and acting as their own proprietors. They were then ever after able to display Off-Broadway programs and ads which they found to be an excellent asset in obtaining other engagements. Then they followed up their letters with phone calls and invitations to see free performances of the production.)

A local Sunday School director saw another play Karen and Celia created for children of their women's group. Would they write and direct a play on a religious theme for his school, he asked. They would and they did. Would they write another?

Recognizing the Activities You Enjoy

By this time, after all the shows they had written and worked with, Karen realized the two things she most enjoyed were working with children and dramatics. If only she could combine the two into some kind of paying career. If only. . . . Eventually she said to herself, "Well, why can't I? But how?"

Yet it was the recognition of what interested her that provided Karen with her solution. Once she knew she wanted children plus dramatics to equal career, the solution followed naturally. Once you isolate what interests you, your equation and solution may also grow naturally from that insight.

"I realized I was already doing what I wanted on a volunteer basis. Why couldn't I move it to a paid career? When the Sunday School director asked for the second play, we hesitated. 'Oh, we'll be glad to pay you,' he said."

If One Institution Will Pay, Maybe Others Will Too

Karen picked up the telephone and tested her new insight. (Celia was uninterested in further work.) Karen called the local Y and asked for an interview. Yes, with her background, they would like to hire her for a once-a-week children's drama group. Next she met with the director of the town recreation program. "A children's summer drama program?" she suggested. Yes, they too were interested. Then another religious school heard of her from the first Sunday school director; then a private high school.

By the time the second religious school called, Karen had almost a year's experience. "I was already being paid quite well by the hour, but this time I took a deep breath and asked for an *additional* $5.00 an hour over what I'd been getting. He agreed instantly. I realized, gee, it's not so hard to ask for what you really think you're worth. That's my price from now on. It's excellent pay by the hour. I work Sunday morning, two afternoons a week, plus whatever evening or weekend time the Tel-A-Story and my advertising and T.V. projects require. I have the freedom to take care of my family and grow in any direction I want. I couldn't do more. Do you realize I have four different plays and scenery and props and casts going through my head at one time?"

Some Things Lead to Others Naturally; Some Things You Help Along

"But how did you go from children's theater to U.H.F. T.V. plays and a toehold in advertising?" I asked.

"A man in an advertising agency saw an ad we ran in *New York* magazine for our Off-Broadway showings. He called us for professionals to play in an advertising skit. Then it developed he needed people to write the skit. That just fell on us. Slowly we've created other advertising, T.V. opportunities by sending out letters and flyers by calling everyone in any way connected with the business we happen to be acquainted with, and buttonholing anyone we meet anywhere who seems to be part of advertising or T.V. Once I got started, one thing just led to another." This from the woman who once feared a smidgin of organizational responsibility!

Premarriage Occupation Plus Volunteer Work Equals the Unexpected

Karen Ostrow added her elementary school training to her volunteer drama work and produced a career that combined the two. You can add premarriage occupation and volunteer activities and find yourself catapulted into a totally new type of work that might never have occurred to you.

For seven years Jeanne Vance struggled to find an interesting part-time job. When her third child entered first grade, she began her search. She believed that eventually her B.A. degree, her prechildren experience as a gal Friday in an advertising agency, and her volunteer executive work would carry her to an interesting editorial or administrative career. Once she was offered an editorial job, full-time. An executive search organization was sufficiently impressed with her credentials to suggest a complex executive search job, full-time. She refused both and returned to her extensive volunteer commitments.

One day she attended a career search forum at her local community college that had advertised interviews for administrative jobs for women. "There were representatives from many area companies there," Jeanne told me. "But the jobs were pitifully few, and there must have been four hundred women milling around. All of them middle-aged, well-dressed, many of them college women, and all after the same thing: an administrative job of some sort, preferably part-time. Finally, after my seven years of sporadic searching, looking at these hundreds of hungry women, it hit me. I was never going to find an interesting part-time administrative job through *traditional* channels. That's what everyone wanted. When an opening for such occurred, it was going to be snapped up by someone on the spot, not advertised. I realized that the only way I would ever find interesting part-time work was by creating it myself."

Insight Equals Job and Career

Once Karen knew that she wanted children and drama to equal a career, it was simple and natural to ask the Sunday school director for payment and thus launch herself. After seven years of floundering, Jeanne's insight that she must create the job herself brought her a career within 20 hours. This is the literal truth. I haven't exaggerated.

"The following afternoon I was sitting at the kitchen table drinking coffee and reading a weekly newspaper which concentrates on community activities for our whole county. On the front page a box mentioned the newspaper was 30 years old and was hoping to continue growing and serving all community organizations. It was signed by the owner. In an instant, with the surety of revelation, I realized this is what I should do, what I could do. I called the owner, explained I'd lived in the county for 20 years, had worked extensively with many community organizations. I told him there were many interesting and important organization stories that never reached his paper. I could cover them and I could also through my organization contacts with people increase subscriptions to his paper.

"I'm positive that if I hadn't concluded I must invent my own opportunity, that newspaper box wouldn't have triggered anything in my brain. Once I knew I'd have to do it myself, I was primed to see the connection between all the volunteer work I'd been doing all those years and an opportunity to use it. Since I was going to work on commission for subscriptions and individual moderate payment for articles, not a weekly salary, he had new subscriptions to gain and nothing to lose by hiring me. So he did."

Businesses, after all, are in business to make money. Any time you can follow Jeanne's approach and show any business of any kind you will make money for it, you have hold of the magic formula for getting the job.

One Plus Two Equals Five

A year later when I interviewed Jeanne, she laughed and said though she was still working for the newspaper and enjoying it immensely, her career had progressed in a direction she would never have foreseen. "I expected to spend most of my time writing news stories and arranging organization, special-price subscriptions. Instead I've drifted into selling commercial ads for the newspaper. [Again to her employer's delight. Ads are the economic lifeblood of publications.] I find to my surprise I prefer it. Now I wouldn't want a confining administrative or editorial job. I like the people-contact of selling, and the time flexibility it gives me is very attractive.

"After all these years of organization work where I learned to deal with people and to talk people into taking on volunteer responsibilities, I've discovered I can use this same skill to approach stores and banks and retail businesses and pleasantly talk them into buying ads, often on the telephone. Every newspaper has different commission rates. I've arranged a very remunerative rate. It's a small paper. Whatever I bring in is more than he'd have without me, so he's willing to give me a good share. I make my own part-time hours, often working at home on the phone. Even a very responsible administrative job wouldn't begin to pay me hour for hour what I'm earning."

"Do you think you could take your experience selling ads to a major newspaper or magazine?" I asked.

"Definitely. I've already had offers. But for the time being what I have is part-time, perfect. I really enjoy it."

Jeanne had known for years that the county newspaper was missing important organization news. Her experience in county organization work told her so. The career connection occurred when she comprehended that *she* was the one who could fill that need.

Your own volunteer work gives you an expertise and in-depth knowledge in some area. It is very possible that on the edge of your consciousness you are aware of needs you could fill—what has ever flitted through your mind as something that "should exist" or "should be taken care of" for your organization or volunteer project. Jeanne saw the weakness in organization news coverage. The magic question she had to put to herself and that you have to put to yourself when you notice one of these needs is:

Well, Why Don't I Fill That Need?

You have to be clear-eyed about what you know. Your natural reaction when you notice a space, a need in your community, is to believe that the need is not filled because "they"—the people in authority, the "experts"—do not think it needs attention. Jeanne Vance's years of experience with a spectrum of community organizations gave her an expertise about what the county newspaper was missing that few people in her county could match. The reason the newspaper continued year in and year out to overlook the stories was not that "they" felt the stories were unimportant, but that "they" didn't know as much about what was happening as Jeanne did! They did not realize the stories were being passed over. When Jeanne showed them how they could both expand their coverage and add to their income, she was enthusiastically welcomed.

It is very possible that your volunteer efforts have given you an insight that no one else has. The lack that you perceive probably exists because you are one of the few people who recognize the problem. All those years of living, participating in that volunteer activity, have given you an understanding of that particular community or volunteer world, which—accept it—may make you a bona fide expert in the subject.

What do you see that "ought to be done"? What service "ought to exist"? Why couldn't you make a career of that?

Letting Them Know They Need You

Jeanne emphasizes, "You have to call or write and offer in these situations as I did [and as Karen did] because the whole point is 'they' don't know they need you! You perceive the need, you realize you can fill it, you seek out the right people and indicate to them what you can do for them. Then you keep growing as one thing leads to another."

The need that Harriet Lefkowith recognized was countywide, and its name was "women."

"Now that is one dumb career idea!" everyone told her when she first suggested it. Even her husband, who has always enthusiastically encouraged her, was temporarily dubious. "How can you make a career out of women?"

Harriet remembers that though her mother was devoted to her work as a millinery buyer for a Pennsylvania department store, Harriet was raised and sent through college during the "Feminine Mystique" era with absolutely no thought she would ever work. "But I discovered I must have a commitment," says Harriet. "I don't play cards. I'm not a sportswoman. When my third and last child entered first grade, I returned to college for a master's in English. I'm a happy student. I love it. If they assigned seven books, I read seventeen. That's the way I throw myself into everything."

In her search for an occupation, Harriet noticed a newspaper ad for Catalyst, the women's organization dedicated to solving problems of part-time employment for educated women. They wanted volunteers. "Of course, I identified with their goals immediately. I had a master's and no place to go with it." As a twice-weekly volunteer at Catalyst, Harriet planned career workshops for women, helped develop written materials for them, interviewed people for jobs or for job information, talked to employers. "I was soon commuting to their office four days a week, reading voraciously on the subject, inventing techniques I needed as I went along, and learning constantly from books and experiences."

Based on her ten months of Catalyst volunteer experience, Harriet noticed a need. "Here I was commuting to the city, and I realized there was absolutely nothing being done for women in our whole suburban county." Then she asked the necessary question: Why can't I fill that need? "I decided to make women my career."

But How Are You Going to Make a Career
Out of a Need Like That?

"I went to one of the largest community adult schools in our area and offered to run a five-session employment workshop for women: how to write a resume, think through options, where to get information, etc. They agreed and paid me for it." [In Section IV we will explore the many other uses to which you can put community adult schools.] Though the enrollment was a meager six, Harriet convinced the school leaders there was a burgeoning nationwide interest in the subject, and the course lived.

Rapidly Harriet invoked the same principle that Karen had used so well and that you can use, too: if one organization or adult school will pay you for your self-created career, why not others? She developed a second course dealing with the literature of the women's movement and made an appointment at a second town's adult school, where she explained the course and sold it. Harriet then sold her women's career workshop to the director of "Weekend College" at a nearby university. Each job took one night a week. A phone call from a woman she had known at Catalyst suggested another direction. The woman now worked at a giant pharmaceutical firm. Would Harriet be interested in creating and running workshops for their secretaries, explaining the new affirmative action laws and the changing roles and expectations of women? If so, she should submit a proposal. (Volunteer work always means you meet people, and they come to know what you can do.)

"So I submitted the proposal, got the job, again once a week."

"Wait!" I interrupted. "How did you know how to write a proposal for a huge corporation? Many women might have been totally stopped by such a request. Didn't it frighten you?"

"Sure it was scary. I'd never written a proposal. But, remember, I'd never done anything else either. I was learning *everything* as I went along. I asked advice from everybody. And I had my contact at the pharmaceutical corporation show me satisfactory proposals others had written for them for other purposes. (In this instance, Adele's and Gloria's system proved itself in a free-lance, commercial context, beginning by following procedures the organization had approved in the past.)

How to Make Opportunity Come to You

As Harriet tells it, you might be beguiled into thinking she was "lucky." Two years after she blanketed the county with her various projects, she attended a luncheon at the state capital celebrating the opening of a State Office on Women. There the dean of community services at Harriet's local community college had a suggestion. Perhaps Harriet might like to direct a Women's Institute at the college? "Let's try it one day a week," the dean suggested.

Within a year, the one day expanded to two and a half. Three years later it was full-time, and Harriet phased out her other courses. Today Harriet is a full-scale executive. She plans, administers, and hires teachers for the Women's Institute's 40 annual courses; she speaks at organizations throughout the county; she's had a promotion to assistant to dean of community services. As assistant, she retains her Women's Institute merry-go-round and also sits on major community committees and helps plan community service courses.

"I don't know where it'll all lead except I want to keep learning and growing." Her face reflected the same joy Karen's had at having created after her fortieth birthday a career that promised "an upward, deliciously unforeseeable path."

Was it luck that caused the dean and Harriet to be together at that meeting? Or was it the kind of luck anyone can arrange for herself? The state capital is 90 miles from Harriet's home. It took effort, not luck, for her to be there. Was it luck that the dean thought to choose Harriet?

Harriet recalls that at that period of her life, "I was everywhere that a woman thing was going on. I was at seminars and conferences and luncheons and giving my community and college corporation courses. Everywhere, trying to do things and see what could happen."

In other words, if the dean had not offered Harriet an opportunity at that particular luncheon, eventually at some other women's meeting a dean of another college or a corporate official or a government official interested in creating a women's center or women's agency would have. By being wherever action for women existed, Harriet saw to it that she was constantly in the "right place."

Under these *self-created* circumstances, it was only a matter of time until it all intersected and she became the right person in the right place at the right time.

"Would the 'unskilled' housewife you were five years ago have believed it was all possible?" I asked.

She shook her head in silent wonder. "I don't think so."

6
With or Without
a College Degree

Learn How to Display Your Volunteer Achievements

Prospective employers often dismiss volunteer activities with an impatient shrug. "If you didn't do it for pay, it's not real work," seems to be their attitude. Since Harriet Lefkowith has worked with thousands of women in her courses and at the Women's Institute, I asked her what techniques she has discovered to solve this problem. A woman's resume, she believes, should be a tool; it should do what the woman wants it to do for her. "Every employment agency and executive search agency has its own methods. Resumes from men follow dozens of different forms. Why shouldn't a woman use the form that suits her needs? Instead of listing jobs or activities which shout 'volunteer,' a woman should list *competencies*. Basically what she's doing is interpreting her volunteer work in business terms. She's using headings like 'administrative experience,' 'sales experience,' 'financial experience,' 'scheduling experience,' and 'personnel experience,' and putting her volunteer achievements under these topics.

Perhaps a woman has headed a town project for the garden club. Her resume might discuss her knowledge this way:

Administrative Experience:
Represented [organization] in arrangements with Town Council. Arranged scope and locale of work with town Parks Commission. Supervised installation to completion.

Financial Experience:
Invited bids and purchased $3,000 worth of trees at 15 percent less than previous year's garden club project costs. Advertised for landscape architect proposals. Negotiated contract with landscape architect at "commercial" not "retail" rates.

In one of the "Women on the Job" columns in *McCall's* magazine, Janice LaRouche, a leading women's career counselor, and her writer-colleague Mary Scott Welch discuss this technique. They use the example of the woman who is annually involved in the book fair at her children's school and consequently has developed skills in buying, pricing, promoting, recruiting of workers, and supervising of sales. Even if she weren't the chairperson of the sale, she would be learning these skills just by being involved. Ms. Welch and Ms. LaRouche point out that other women might be able to report something like the following:

Profits of thrift shop increased 40 percent inflation discounted under my direction. . . . My presentation of our committee goals (copy attached) won us a citizen's award from the *Herald* and persuaded the "Friends of New Albion" to provide matching fund grants to carry out the reform program outlines. . . . As a result of the publicity campaign, which I headed, the cooperative day-care center, formerly housed in our members' private homes on a rotating volunteer basis, now occupies permanent space and has a paid staff of two. . . .

Without claiming sole responsibility for such results, these statements show that you understand how to present your accomplishments in terms your employer can relate to—not with the one-sided passion of a do-gooder but with the cool recitation of measurable facts.

However, organizing your volunteer credits properly will help only if you also project a serious sense of purpose when you go for a job interview. Creating an aura of looking for a job in order to "fill my time" or in order to have something "pleasant and interesting" to do is self-defeating. One senior executive put it this way: "I'm not running an adult camp in order to keep women amused with 'interesting' jobs. I'm running a business for which I need people who will concentrate on what they can offer the business and who will be seriously committed to their jobs and their responsibilities. I don't need someone who will take the job today, work for six months, and then quit to go on a cruise." Not everyone may be as blunt as this executive, but all employers share that attitude. They will all be measuring you for that businesslike quality as they talk to you.

Packaging

When I interviewed Pat Dimitri (we will meet Pat in detail in Section III), she recalled that in the years before she held any college degrees, she and three friends once headed a women's club volunteer project that taught English to foreign-born hospital interns. Because these interns were educated people, far above the schooling level of most immigrants, all the existing materials used to teach English to foreigners were inappropriate. Pat and her friends collected every text they could find, interviewed professors, pored over texts on the techniques of teaching language and ultimately created a totally new course complete with numerous classroom exercises for teaching English to educated foreigners. Pat sighed when she told me about it. "Back in those preliberation days it never occurred to us to do anything with our creation. One professor I showed the materials to was openly impressed. He said there was nothing else in existence to meet that need. Now I realize we could easily have packaged our program and gone into business selling it to hospitals all over our area. Probably we could even have gotten a book contract to write a text. But then women never thought of such things. Because we didn't have college degrees of our own, we didn't have the courage to realistically appraise what we had self-taught ourselves. Besides, we had swallowed the brainwashing and thought of ourselves as "only volunteers." Therefore, how could our project be important? Now I'd have the courage with or without a college degree."

Self-Taught Knowledge and How You Can Use It

Dr. Henry W. Wriston, president emeritus of Brown University, has evaluated *self-taught knowledge of any kind and how you can use it.* He describes how as a young scholar he found he was unemployable.

> I was a medievalist, and there was less than no demand for someone to teach youth about the Middle Ages. So I manufactured a job for which I had no training whatever. I got paid to write a book on how to raise money from the public. The volume was not high literature but it put bread on the table and led, many years later, to my appointment to a group of five to organize the National War Fund during the Second World War.
>
> Writing that book proved to me that I could do something without specific training. That is true of most people who have not been so indoctrinated that they believe they must run in a groove. . . .

The housewives we have been discussing in this book all have in common that, like Dr. Wriston, they have created jobs and careers for which they had no *formal* training. They taught themselves their skills or learned them as volunteers, then gradually crystalized them in their paid jobs.

Until World War II most men's training for their careers was self-obtained and acquired on the job. Abraham Lincoln, like most lawyers, read law himself and learned while he clerked. To this day some states admit to the bar anyone who has clerked and is able to pass the state bar examination, be his book-learning self-taught or gained at Harvard. Did John D. Rockefeller and John Wanamaker and their business colleagues go to business school? Who taught Thomas Edison and his contemporaries engineering? From what journalism school did H. L. Mencken, Heywood

Broun, or Alexander Woollcott graduate? And which fashion institute claims Coco Chanel as an alumna? In recent years all the practitioners of new industries like T.V. and film—directors, announcers, performers, camera people, makeup, artists, and lighting experts—have learned on the job. Only when an industry becomes established and crowded are formal educational barriers erected.

The formal educational barriers are useful as devices to help sort through the glut of applicants and limit the press of bodies toward jobs. But their value as sifters has become muddled in the public mind. Formal training has come to mean the only way to learn the vocation. One way to learn the vocation, yes. The only way? Certainly not. An excellent case can be developed for the premise that a combination of some technical texts and on-the-spot experience still yields the most skill and savvy. It is important for your confidence, when you think of inventing and developing a career, to recognize what you have already accomplished during your years of living and what you now know as a result of these experiences. With or without a formal college label, as Jeanne, Karen, Pat, and Harriet discovered, you know what you know.

This Book's Basic Promise Confirmed: An Interesting Job Immediately

When you invent a career, you often bypass the formal education barrier. Because this career is newly invented by you, there are no formal educational requirements. That is why you can fulfill the initial promise of this book: to leap up the career ladder to an exciting important position rather than start at the bottom as the "experts" have been insisting you must do. Harriet was able to step into the directorship of the college's Women's Institute because this is, as T.V. and film were, a new occupation. New occupations very sensibly set ability to perform as their basic criterion.

When enough Women's Institutes are functioning in this

country and enough people begin clamoring to administer them, applicants will outstrip jobs. Then we will begin to see the development of degree requirements and the flourishing of such courses as "Techniques of Administering Women's Institutes."

Karen was able to obtain educational positions with the town's recreation commission, two Sunday schools, a private state-accredited high school, and the local Y youth program. Eventually, when enough talented women and men seek drama-teaching posts with their school systems, barriers will be erected. Applicants will discover they must complete a certain number of college credits in drama beyond their teaching certificates before being considered. But now—now—as you discover a need, you are the pioneer in that occupation, the person who is qualified to do it on practical knowledge alone (even if you are making up and discovering that knowledge day by day as you go along).

But I'm Too Old to Start

To counter the middle-aged feeling that it is too late to start a new career and accomplish anything, Dr. Wriston continues:

> Years ago just for the fun, I made a study of careers. To my astonishment I found most "successful" men changed their occupations in middle life. . . . The alteration is frequently not only radical but accidental. One career derailed and a new one is found. . . .

Dr. Wriston is discussing men. Yet have you ever read a more accurate description of a homemaker's life pattern? At middle age "one career is derailed" as her children grow up. Why can't you make the rest of Dr. Wriston's analysis apply to you? "I found most 'successful' men changed their occupations in middle life. . . . The alteration is frequently not only radical but accidental. . . ."

"Accidental" perhaps, but accidental only in the sense that these people had, during their years of living, unconsciously been developing competencies for the new occupation. Take your competencies and do the same.

With no college degree and no relevant previous work experience, Marian Burden did just that. On a typical day as director of public relations for a huge suburban branch of Bloomingdale's, a major New York–based department store, you will find Marian greeting her guest—Julia Child, perhaps—at 9:00 A.M. She will introduce Ms. Child to 400 people packed into Bloomingdale's chic restaurant. When Ms. Child leaves at about 11:30 after her talk, demonstration, and book autographing, Marian will be busy arranging for future guests—as many as three or four per week—for instance, clothes designer Pauline Trigère, socialite-editor Wyatt Cooper, and authorities in the arts and the musical theater. Since 50 percent of her work involves the county's numerous women's volunteer organizations, she will probably spend time that day discussing fund-raising plans with organization leaders. She will see to press coverage for her various programs and juggle details of in-store affairs for the 500 employees (it is a very big store). Today may also feature one of her many in-store promotions. Perhaps Marian has arranged for a backgammon expert to visit the store for several hours of playing and explanation. Through this activity and the circulars, posters, and press coverage that Marian will generate about it, she will be calling customers' attention to Bloomingdale's game department. That evening Marian may contribute effort and knowledge as board member of a community volunteer organization as she represents the store in the community.

Volunteer Work Alone Can Equal Great Paid Career

Says Marian, "The volunteer work I did for 22 years was very similar to what I've been doing for 8 years as public relations director. The only real difference is as a volunteer I wasn't paid."

For the 22 years while she raised her four sons, Marian worked for the Presbyterian Church's Women's Church Guild, the women's auxiliary of the Junior Chamber of Commerce ("In

Omaha, Nebraska, where we lived, it was called 'The Better Halves' "), Federated Garden Clubs, various dance, library, and choral groups, and two hospital auxiliaries. Everywhere she built organizations, recruited board members and speakers for programs, publicized, raised funds, and administered. Through it all she was unconsciously honing her native talent for empathizing and getting along with people. *Any woman who has successfully worked with many organizations has probably developed strong interpersonal skills.*

The courses in journalism and business that Marian took "were marvelously useful in all my volunteer work. But it was the actual doing in the volunteer activities that made me grow and gave me the insights and capabilities I use in my job today." Any woman with volunteer experiences has grown and learned.

Bloomingdale's was searching for a woman in her late 30s or early 40s. They felt that was the perfect age. (Still think 40 is too old?) They wanted someone with extensive volunteer experience to work with women's volunteer organizations as liaison to the community, someone who would know how to relate to organizations and understand their interests and goals.

"I hadn't the faintest interest in a job. I'd just chaired a very successful church fair which produced wide publicity. A friend who worked for the store called and urged me to apply. [As with Harriet, this can hardly be called "luck." Because of all her volunteer activities, Marian had inevitably impressed many people with her capabilities. If you've been successfully carrying out volunteer assignments, you have also inevitably impressed people.]

"What would you do if you held the public relations position?" Marian was asked during her interview.

"In fifteen minutes I gave a capsule view of what could be done over a period of years. For 22 years I had been the representative of volunteer organizations, going to businesses trying to obtain donations and support for our fund-raising projects. I knew what a store had to do to produce a positive response. They offered me the job. Now my schedules of guest programs are one of my major activities. I've arranged it so women's organizations use these programs as fund-raisers. The organizations sell tickets and keep all proceeds. The constant traffic of potential new customers brought into the store when the organization members come for the programs is my evidence of successful public relations." Marian's guest-calendar concept has been so successful that every store in the chain has adopted the system.

Other Ways to Translate Volunteer Work Straight into a Great Career

I asked Marian how other women with volunteer experience doing publicity for organizations might find part-time or full-time jobs. "I know women who have built [invented] wonderful part-time public relations positions for themselves by going into a place—a restaurant, health spa, small retail store—and analyzing it. For example, the restaurant might have a good dinner crowd and be very slow at lunch. A woman can go in, analyze its assets, think of promotions and ideas she could use to bring people and groups into that restaurant to publicize it. Then go to the owner and suggest she do the job. Even if the owner claims there's no budget to pay her or offers only a tiny fee, the woman should go ahead. Do the work and prove what she can accomplish. When she's had some success, the owner may be willing to pay her or she can use these successes elsewhere to impress and win other clients. I know women who've done it.

"Publicity is a good deal more than ads in newspapers. Most women who've successfully worked for organizations haven't had money for ads. They've accomplished things and publicized their group's efforts with their wits. That's what will be their asset in devising a public relations job. They can also compile a portfolio of their volunteer publicity and take it to a public relations firm to obtain a position there."

What Clientele Could You Bring?

"Another woman I know developed her volunteer work directly into a very different kind of business career," said Marian. "She'd been very active in church work, Boy Scouts, country vacations for underprivileged children. She's a very pretty woman with a good figure and she often modeled in fashion shows for these groups. Gradually she added to her modeling. She organized the shows, coordinated clothes and accessories, ran the shows for the organizations. When she decided she wanted a paid job, she visited an elegant boutique that she'd worked with on fashion shows. They were delighted to hire her as a fashion coordinator. She knew fashion, and her many contacts within organizations meant she could act as sales and show liaison with them and bring a new clientele to the boutique—which she did. Why couldn't other women with good volunteer backgrounds do the same?" This is a totally different aspect of Jeanne Vance's realization that her volunteer contacts could help her make money for the newspaper by increasing the paper's subscription list, thus making her services attractive to an employer.

The same "clientele" principle in another guise operates within Marian's suggestions about public relations. Since a P.R. firm's ability to serve its clients and so make money depends directly on the people it has access to, a woman with wide volunteer contacts would be a very valuable addition to a public relations group—if she brings her talent to their attention in her resume.

The travel business is a self-employed way to apply the volunteer clientele principle. Beginners' pay in travel work is relatively low. Consequently, established agencies are constantly taking on apprentices. Once you know the business, you can move out on your own. Then all the personal contacts of your volunteer days become a rich source of organizational and individual travel clientele.

What kind of job would you enjoy where your volunteer acquaintances would be welcomed as a new group of potential customers for that business? As soon as you have the answer, you have the most powerful job-getting credential of them all, the ability to provide new customers for your prospective employer. Where is there an employer who will be able to resist that lure and you?

"A third woman I know," Marian continued, "had been active with a few volunteer interests while her children were young. Nothing spectacular, just keeping busy. When she needed college money for them, she took a job with computers with the phone company. Within a year she'd been promoted three times and was earning nearly twice what she'd earned when she was first hired."

I interrupted. "I don't understand the connection with her volunteer work. Surely she wasn't working with computers as a volunteer."

Marian smiled. "Don't you see it doesn't matter whether the job you eventually take spins off directly from your volunteer work or not? If you're serious about your paid job, then you'll find that those years of volunteer activities kept your brain alive, kept your abilities alive. When you go into paid work, you'll be ready to go and succeed."

SECTION III

EXPERIENCE HELPING YOUR HUSBAND WITH HIS JOB OR BUSINESS CAN START YOU IN THE MIDDLE OR AT THE TOP

Why a through-your-husband section? Isn't developing a career through your husband contrary to the ideas of women as individuals in their own right? No, it is a realistic way of salvaging what is by fitting it to the new. Many women who arranged their lives to suit the old sex-role patterns now find themselves stranded in their 30s, 40s, or 50s with no career training, no job experience.

Since we cannot go back and undo the years during which a woman effaced her own interests and devoted herself exclusively to applauding or aiding her husband's career, we are now going to try to turn the situation around. We are going to make her everyday experiences during those years yield a great career for her. This section tells how.

1
When You "Had to" Help Your Husband

When Eloise Garrity's four children were young, she used to say that going to the basement to do the daily family laundry was a lot more complicated than it looked. At first glance it was an ordinary suburban laundry room with cinderblock walls, lit by a few naked ceiling bulbs, and on the floor a carpet remnant strewn with playpen, wagons, toys, plastic geegaws, and assorted other necessities of four children ages one, three, five, and nine. But the daylight which might have filtered through the small basement windows was blocked by boards Phil Garrity had used to partition one-half the area into a crude business office. With another corner occupied by furnace and hot water heater, Eloise, the children, and the washing equipment had to survive as best they could in the remaining corner of what she called her "Ohio Black Hole of Calcutta."

"It was the constant phone calls and business details for Phil that really made it hard," says Eloise. "I'd be doing the wash, taking care of the children, and at the same time have two phone calls for Phil's business on hold and a third call I was talking to."

Because there are approximately 400,000 new businesses founded each year in the United States, millions of American homemakers like Eloise Garrity have developed wide job and career skills while helping their husband with these enterprises. It is axiomatic that husband and wife work long and hard for most fledgling companies. Usually they can afford very little sales, administrative, clerical, and all-around factotum help other than themselves.

Women like Eloise who have helped their husbands with businesses (even if the businesses ultimately fail) have usually learned in depth the skills they will need to command high salaried, paid positions *if they realize what they have to offer.*

After ten years as a plumbing supply salesman, Eloise's husband, Phil, had quit his job and set up a plumbing sales company of his own. The customers he wooed and sometimes won were retail home-supply centers, hardware supermarkets, and real estate developers. With Phil away most of the day stalking customers, Eloise was left in her basement laundry/office to cope with suppliers' and customers' phone calls.

In order to survive, Eloise learned how to cut through red tape and expedite orders from suppliers to customers. She learned how to soothe a customer and solve a crisis. Most important, she learned to do four things at once and to cope with the unforeseen and the difficult. In the evening quiet after the children were bedded, she learned to help Phil with bookkeeping, record keeping, order forms, tax forms, tax regulations, bank loan forms, bank regulations.

For three years Phil drove himself 18 hours a day. At the end of three years there were no more credit lines available, too many debts, and too few customers. Phil was forced to abandon the effort. He returned to a payroll and the family tagged along.

Phil tore down the basement office partition, finished the area into a family playroom. Eloise drifted into volunteer work for Little League and the school P.T.A., usually craft activities and hospitality for various of the organizations' functions. Three years after their business failure, when their oldest child was 15, Eloise recalls, "It hit me that we were soon going to have four children going through college, and I'd better start earning some extra money for that and for all the trips and other things we'd always wanted. Or we'd never have any of them! I had a year and a half of college and then worked as a secretary for three years before the children were born. I liked college. I was always good at school, but twenty years ago things were different. My parents kept nagging me to quit. They told me I'd be too educated to ever find a husband and that college was a waste of time for a girl."

When You Have to Get a Job Fast: Confidence Building

"Anyway, I had the three years secretarial experience before the children, and I'd done the secretarial work for Phil's business. I figured if I was going to work to make money, then I ought to make money. I wanted a good, responsible office job that would pay well. But after all these years I was terrified of trying for a high-paying position. I take a size fourteen dress, not an eight the way I used to. And don't offices want cute young things?" Her square, lightly freckled face crinkled reflectively as she sent that rhetorical question in my direction.

Eventually, like many other women trying to move from home to paid work, Eloise nervously registered at one of the office-temporary agencies in her neighborhood. "Eloise's anxieties are typical," says Dorothy Becker, a corporate vice-president of Staff Builders, one of the large national temporary personnel firms. Over the 15 years during which Mrs. Becker has risen from part-time interviewer to vice-president, she has noticed that "many women settle into clerical jobs far below their real abilities because they don't realize they are well able to hold a more interesting job and earn more. By beginning with temporary opportunities, they gain confidence and a wider view of the kinds of work that are available. After only a few weeks of fumbling and anxiety and making a few mistakes, they begin to believe they can function and that they are worth a good day's wages. Then they're ready to tackle the employment world with a much higher opinion of themselves."

This description certainly matches Eloise's progress. After three months she began scanning the full-time want ads. "I'd discovered I certainly could type. My shorthand was adequate. If necessary, I could have taken a quick shorthand refresher course. I'd learned to use the new dictaphones and other new office machines on the various temporary jobs. Then I started wanting to belong somewhere. I wanted familiar people to lunch with every day, people I could get to know. You can't build an office social relationship on a constantly changing temporary basis."

After weeks of answering ads—"I must have gone to ten interviews"—Eloise was still jobless. "Every day our local newspaper had a whole flock of ads for gal Fridays or for 'secretary, challenging, creative position, must be able to self-start, manage own responsibilities, salary and fringes high.' There were certainly plenty of good secretarial jobs." Eloise's personal observation is true of the entire United States. The supply of competent secretaries nowhere equals demand. Demand so far exceeds supply that companies often provide inducements over and above attractive salaries. Open your local newspaper and notice how almost every ad for a secretary emphasizes delightful surroundings to work in, fringe benefits, pleasant social contacts, all as extra bait to attract competent applicants. "Yet with all the ads, nothing happened at the really good jobs. I'd tell them I worked as a secretary before my children were born. I'd even say I helped my husband with his business. No one hired me. After a while I decided the high-paying offices did want cute young chicks. I got so the thought of going for an interview would make me nauseous. I stopped. I'm not the kind of person who can go on a crash diet or make myself over in some fantastic way. People tell me I dress nicely. I'm not 22 and it's silly to try to pretend to look it.

"Then one day there was an ad that really spelled out what they wanted. Usually ads for better pay, interesting secretarial jobs, just say things like 'self-starters, customer skills.' I'd never been able to convince any of these employers. This ad said, 'Administrative secretary to sales manager. Good secretarial skills and experience dealing with suppliers, customers, expediting, record keeping, telephone sales relations, able to deal with crises.' Well, of course, that's exactly what I did for Phil—while coping with four children besides! I sat down, wrote them a letter. I took their list of what they wanted and told them exactly what I'd done in each category. They called. I got my courage together, went for the interview, and was hired.

"Now I realized my fatal mistake in previous interviews was not spelling out what I'd done. I'd say things like 'I helped my husband run his business office,' expecting the employer to know what I meant. This ad gave me the idea of specifically listing my experience. Once I showed them I'd done a very kind of task they had in mind, they wanted me."

Seymour J. Fader, Professor of Management at Ramapo

College, a business consultant and lecturer, and former corporate vice-president, explains that one of the most valuable job-interview techniques consists of learning *how to describe* your past work experience. When applying for any job, you will usually find a space for "Past Positions Held." During an interview you will have to talk about your past experience. Says Professor Fader, "Adults as well as teen-agers take our college business courses. They're constantly coming to professors for help obtaining jobs. In talking to them, I find women and men as well as youngsters often fail to explain their work experience properly. The women in particular, as Eloise did, sell themselves short." One middle-aged woman came to Professor Fader recently and told him that four years as a salesgirl in the hosiery-novelty department of her local department store represented her total employment record. Yes, she was still employed, but selling hosiery and accessories didn't seem much of a recommendation for anything else.

"Are selling and wrapping hosiery and accessories the only things you've done on the job?" asked Professor Fader. "Tell me everything you ever do there."

The Right Way to List Your Past Work Experience

Haltingly, the list tumbled out. The woman totaled cash receipts at the end of each day, kept the department inventory records, hired new girls for the department, and trained them. On the floor manager's day off or when the manager was sick, on vacation, or away buying, the woman acted as department manager, made decisions, saw that displays were taken care of, reorders were sent in, and new supplies were on hand. Besides all that, she added, "Sometimes when other departments are very busy, I do some of the same work for men's wear or woman's junior sports."

That list of job experience is quite different from simply presenting herself as "salesgirl, hosiery department." With her knowledge of hiring and training new girls, she had a background that might lead her to a job with a store, office, or factory personnel or job-training department. With her administrative experience overseeing the department during the manager's absences, she could logically apply for various office and store supervisory positions. Even her department record-keeping and sales supervision suggested possibilities of bookkeeping and payroll work. By applying the same system of *analyzing and listing* all the different activities a woman has performed *in past jobs and in helping her husband with his work,* a woman helps an employer *understand clearly* what her experience is. Then, he sees in her, middle-aged or not, someone valuable who knows how to do the job he wants done, and whom he therefore wants.

In the four years she has been at her job as administrative secretary, Eloise has received two handsome pay increases. "My boss says he doesn't know how he'd manage without me. Temporary work restored my skills and confidence. Dealing with customers and crises is like riding a bicycle. Once you learn, you never forget. Since then I've noticed how many women in their 30s, 40s, 50s hold down the higher-level office positions. They may want cute young things at reception desks and other light-duty areas. For the higher responsibility, better-pay spots, they're often happy to have a competent woman who's been around long enough to know something."

Where the Fat Paychecks Are

The salary-scale Bible, *Office Salaries: Directory for United States and Canada,* based on the office salaries of more than half a million employees in more than 7,000 companies in 129 major American cities, makes clear the salary differential between routine secretarial jobs and what they call "Secretary A" work. According to the directory, in routine (Secretary B) jobs the employee "performs secretarial duties for middle management . . . limited in area of responsibility. . . ." In Secretary A positions, by contrast, the employee "performs secretarial duties for top-level executive or person responsible for major functional or geographic operations. Does work of confidential nature, *relieves principal of designated administrative details. Requires initiative, judgment, knowledge of company practices, policy, and organization* [emphasis mine.]"

The woman who has learned these Secretary A self-starting

techniques while helping her husband with his work can land the remunerative A positions, if only she realizes what she has to offer! Salaries vary from city to city, as cost-of-living scales vary between cities. The differential remains approximately the same. For Secretary A there is 15 to 20 percent more in the pay envelope each week, together with more interesting work.

Eloise Garrity is happy to continue as an administrative secretary. Other women who are interested in executive work can use high-level secretarial positions as excellent springboards. With legal and moral pressure on companies to promote women, many businesses are frantic to locate qualified women. The woman who has already obtained a thorough grasp of company affairs while working for that firm, can be the ideal candidate *if* she makes clear her ambitions to her superiors. One woman who began as a secretarial administrative assistant in a real estate office gradually took on more and more selling responsibility. Five years after she arrived, she officially became the vice-president of sales. Another housewife, who began as a secretary to the president of a bank, is now the manager of one of the bank's suburban branches. Today, these are not unusual situations.

Unfortunately, many women still play mental hopscotch. They tend to skip over their relevant job experience, thinking of it only in terms of back there, what they did before the children were born. By learning instead to examine what they did during the tumultuous years when they simultaneously raised a family and perhaps helped run their husband's business, they can reach out and grasp a high-level, remunerative position, which can then, if they wish, lead to further promotions.

2
Learning Your Husband's Business on Purpose

When You Want More Than a Salary

If Eloise Garrity's laundry room was once a "suburban Black Hole of Calcutta," Heidi Friedman's may be a suburban American dream come true. When I arrived, Heidi pointed to a heap of ironing in the middle of her elegant family room. After 14 years of marriage, Heidi's spacious, well-furnished suburban house and the two late-model cars in the driveway reflect the family's comfortable income.

As Heidi ironed, I asked the obvious question: "What made you look for a job?"

"I'm the kind of person who isn't happy unless she's busy and involved," Heidi told me. "When my children were little, I really had my fill of charity organization work. I was super-involved with all kinds of causes. When my children were in school full-time, I was ready for something else." In her mid-30s, Heidi is a beautiful woman with the eyes and skin of a Revlon-ad model.

"I can no longer go back to teaching," Heidi explained. "Teaching is so overcrowded there aren't any jobs. Besides it really doesn't interest me anymore. But if I wasn't going to teach, there's not another thing in the world anyone would give me a job for. So I decided to work for my husband."

Learning Your Husband's Business on Purpose

(If your husband does not own a business, everything that follows would apply equally well to learning your father's, mother's, brother's, brother-in-law's, sister's, cousin's, or friend's business on purpose.)

Said Heidi, "I figured if I'm going to work, I might as well put my efforts where they'd help my husband and our family. I also figured it would add to our common interests and be an added bond in our marriage, and it certainly is.

"My husband and his brother run the family business in New York City's garment industry. They do Schiffli embroidery for clothing manufacturers. That's not trimmings. Our kind of embroidery is much more complex. It's all over fabrics, or spot embroidery when you have a design or flower or something on a garment. Until I decided to become a saleswoman for them, *there had never been a woman salesperson in the embroidery trade,* as far as I know.

"My father-in-law started the business thirty years ago. They have forty machine operators and six salespeople, who go out for orders from dress, sweater, suit, and blouse manufacturers. When I started, I figured they'll just pay me commission, no salary. That way I won't cost the company anything while I'm learning. I won't be a drain on the business, and any orders I get are gravy. Eventually I'll learn, and I'll be worth a good salary to my husband or to any company in the field."

The Big Difference Between Heidi's Sales Work and Most Women's Sales Jobs

Mention "woman" and "sales job," and what mental image appears in your mind? A woman behind a counter in a store. A woman doing telephone sales soliciting. These are the bottom rungs of the sales world, providing the lowest pay, usually near the legal minimum, stiff working hours that almost always include some weekend and evening work, fifty weeks a year with little or no flexibility for family responsibilities, children's school vacations, and illnesses. For the woman who has proved herself in family life and perhaps organizational work, there is very little, if any, opportunity to use initiative and executive ability. It is simply a cog-in-a-wheel occupation.

Now mention "man" and "sales job," and what mental image flashes into your mind? Probably a man carrying a sample case, calling on customers in offices and factories. The man is an expert in the occupation he represents. He earns a family income that can range from good to sensational from salary, salary plus commission, or even commission alone. This whole world of real sales, real excitement, real money possibilities, and real opportunities for using one's intelligence is the sales world into which Heidi has leapt.

Any woman with an interest in people and skill in social relations can use her husband's or any relative's or friend's business, as Heidi did, to ease herself into the sky's-the-limit world of real selling. This is a sales life that also offers what Heidi describes as "a chance to be part of the creative process, of eventually helping design products to meet your customers' needs, of being asked for ideas by technicians who produce your product, troubleshooting for customers, being totally involved. *Yet having it all on a flexible daily work schedule you arrange to suit yourself!"*

If, like Heidi, you are willing to work *on commission only* while you are learning, *you are potentially a 100 percent asset* to your husband or relative or friend. If you don't sell anything that week or month, you cost them nothing. As soon as you sell, you have opened a new territory and gained new customers for the company. They have nothing to lose and a new salesperson with an active new sales territory to gain. *Why wouldn't they give you a chance to learn the business under these circumstances?*

But There Has Never Been a Woman Salesperson in the Business

That there has never been a woman salesperson in your relative's or friend's business can be an asset, says Heidi. "You're a first, and it can help you. I went out canvassing cold. The company's regular salesmen were already servicing the regular customers. I had to develop a clientele of my own. My husband gave me a suitcase of samples and said, 'Get yourself a copy of *Women's Wear Daily,* pick out names, and go.' He was very supportive and encouraging. He and my in-laws thought it was fabulous I wanted to try. But he works twelve hours a day, six days a week, very hard, and there wasn't much else he could do to get me started.

"When I called companies and asked for appointments, being a woman was a help. No one had ever heard of a woman salesperson in embroidery. People were curious. I got appointments easily. When I showed up, if the designer or buyer was a woman, we were instantly on the same wavelength of women holding a job while taking care of homes. Even unmarried women are usually running homes. And the men buyers seemed to be pleased with the novelty of a woman selling instead of just another guy."

Since the early 1970s, newspaper reports of the entire American scene have confirmed Heidi's personal observations that a woman salesperson can fare very well in an industry that has been exclusively male. In a long feature story, *The New York Times* profiled Stella Wilson, a Xerox customer representative, who had to battle hard for the chance to sell. Imagine a *woman* renting and selling complicated, prestigious machinery, then having to cope with customer machine-breakdown crisis! Given the chance, Stella began her canvassing cold, starting at the top of office buildings and working her way down. At the time the article was written, she had become New York City's top Xerox sales representative, responsible for a territory running from 54th to 57th streets, from Lexington to Park avenues. Her success in producing higher annual billings than any other New York Xerox representative encouraged the company to hire additional saleswomen.

Other reports recount women's success in car sales, in industrial real estate, heavy machinery, cattle auctioning, and other businesses. A man I know, who holds a degree in electrical engineering, sells sophisticated electronic parts to manufacturers of electronic equipment. He tells me that lately he has become accustomed to meeting competing women sales personnel as he makes his rounds. Most of the women do not have engineering degrees. They cannot sell the really complex items, but, says he, they do very, very well with the rest of their lines.

And why not? People-contact skills, social skills, and flexibility are talents most women develop to a high degree during their years as mothers, wives, neighbors, and volunteers for religious, community, and cultural organizations. If a woman then takes these skills and learns the techniques of selling, she can succeed. I interviewed Heidi three years after she first picked up her suitcase of samples and set forth. In retrospect she believes she could have succeeded faster if she had gone to a community college or any suitable career institute and taken a course in the *techniques* of selling. "It took me a long time to learn to 'close a deal' " she said. "I didn't know how to move from friendly talk and customer interest to pinning them down and getting an order in black and white. Now I do. I had to learn every step of selling slowly by myself through trial and error. A faster, better way might have been that course. A course might also have given me more confidence, which is an inner quality that people can sense with salespeople. I had to develop that gradually."

In addition to courses, there are also many good sales technique books you can study by yourself. One excellent book written for community college sales classes is *Professional Selling* by B. Robert Anderson, published by Prentice-Hall, 1976.

What Kept Her Going?

When I had first telephoned Heidi to ask for an interview appointment, she had been anxious to cooperate. Yet it had taken her several weeks to find time. "I've become so busy with orders and customers that lately I've been working four days a week just keeping up. All the groundwork I did during the beginning months is now bringing in orders.

"For months I didn't sell anything," Heidi told me when we met. "I enjoyed it anyway. My children were only seven and nine when I started. I'd go to New York twice a week. Get there at ten, leave at two, so I'd be back when the children came from school. Counting lunch time, when people don't work, it really came to only six hours a week work, plus maybe two more hours on the phone from home making appointments, keeping up contacts. It was fun. I knew I'd eventually break through. Even though I wasn't making sales I was with the people, out of the house, talking, socializing. Selling of this kind is really developing friendships where people gradually realize they can rely on you to be there, to have the product, to produce on time. For example, one designer I was trying to sign as a customer told me one day she had bought a pet skunk and didn't know where to get it deodorized. A week later my husband and I went away for a weekend, and can you believe it, there I met a woman who had just had a skunk deodorized. Quick as a flash I got the veterinarian's name, sent the buyer a postcard. The next time I called on that buyer, well, of course, we were real friends."

Personal Advantages of This Kind of Selling

Heidi pointed out that selling on a commission-only basis for husband or relative has many advantages. "If my children are sick, do I have to worry about explaining to my employer? He's their father. He's the first to say, 'Cancel your calls. Stay home, take care of them.' It also makes me feel good to be working with my husband. He's under so much business pressure. Now I can better understand. And his support and faith in me when I was learning meant so much.

"From the customers' viewpoint, I see as soon as I tell them my husband owns the business, they consider it an advantage. They feel I have the inside track to get their order done quickly, that I have a personal stake in seeing the work is done properly and the business's reputation is upheld. By now I know far more than just selling. I know all kinds of information about the business in general, including technical knowledge of coloration, dyes, fabrics, stitches, what embroiders well, what doesn't. I could find a job anywhere in the industry."

"Do you think you'll want to stay with sales?" I asked.

She laughed. "My secret dream is to be an archaeologist. But I'm a realist. I know my priorities. They are my husband and children first. There is no way I can go on field work and do the things I'd have to for an archaeology degree and still be here in suburbia as their wife and mother. I'd rather be their wife and mother. As I go deeper into the business, I'm caught up in its complexities. I find it ever more interesting. Now I go on buying trips to Europe with my husband. There are many fascinating aspects of *any* business."

And What Do You Do When People Want to
Mix Sex and Business?

In the *Times* interview with Xerox saleswoman Stella Wilson, writer Judy Klemesrud asked the good-looking Ms. Wilson, a former model, how she dealt with "passes." Her answer was that "very, very few men," make passes at her. The question surfaces in almost everyone's mind as soon as you begin discussing sending women as salespeople into an overwhelmingly masculine buying world. Since the reputation of New York City's garment industry for mixing sex with business is second only to that of Hollywood's, I decided I might as well ask. Heidi shook her head. "Kidding about sex is the number-one topic. It's just kidding. Just fun. No one, not one person has ever made a pass at me. I guess they just sense they can't. I think people respond in business just as they would at a cocktail party. If a woman means 'no,' people sense it. It's just not a problem."

3
Accidentally Inventing
a Great Career for Yourself
by Helping Your Husband

"The thing that absolutely amazes me is that I was perfectly happy at the time," Pat Dimitri told me. She shook her head in astonishment. "Now I think about it and know I could have had so much more so easily. Then I didn't see it. How could I have behaved and thought the way I did? Brainwashed, absolutely brainwashed, that's what I was." If you are between 35 and 70 you will probably recognize some of your own experiences in Pat's. She and I were seated in her high-rise condominium apartment. The building was new. Like Pat and her husband, many of the tenants were in their 40s and 50s, still supporting children in college but able to divest themselves of the chores of suburban homeowning.

The building elevator had brought me to a carpeted hall, then a few steps to Pat's apartment with a magnificent glass-walled living room. As we sank into a billowy beige couch on a white rug, Pat commented, "After bringing up three boys, my husband, Larry, and I and our beaten-up furniture were ready for a change. These things were bought on a tight budget, but they're a new look for us and we enjoy it." With her short curly hair and small-boned body, Pat appears considerably younger than the 50 years she claims.

"Back then before I married, I was going to college at night, working by day," Pat told me. "I'd finished two years of college and loved it. But I quit immediately when I married. Now I ask myself why. My husband didn't push me into it. I've discussed this with other women. It never entered our minds that there were alternatives. As we saw it, we were moving into a new stage of life: marriage. Our job now was the role of housewife. I was supposed to devote myself to a home, husband, and eventually children. I was already earning money from a job; why did I think I had to quit college?"

It was not until years later, after her sons were born and her husband had completed his master's degree, that Pat decided, "Eventually my time will come." That time arrived when her youngest entered first grade. "Even then I didn't see it clearly," she admits. "I wanted a college degree in social work. In the 1960s, teaching, library, nursing, and social work were about the only professions anybody thought of for women. The local college offered only teaching. It didn't occur to me or to any of my friends that with a little driving I could have attended another college that did feature social work. We didn't yet see women's occupations as important enough to fuss about. I'd had some very satisfactory experiences in volunteer activities that involved teaching English to foreign doctors. So I studied teaching."

You Probably Know More Than You Think You Know

For most of their marriage, Pat's husband, Larry, has been market research director for a large food-canning company. It is Larry's responsibility to find out what consumers like, do not like, will buy, will not buy, and why. Over the years he has developed new market research techniques to suit his special needs. During those years, he and Pat often lingered over dinner or weekend breakfast discussing, analyzing, and developing his new ideas.

No matter what a man's occupation is, if he and his wife are at all compatible, his wife—like Pat—will hear about, discuss, and ultimately know a good deal about her husband's job. She will know from their daily "What happened at work today?" and from weekend socializing, which so often includes work buddies. The career trick for a woman is to *realize* she has considerable knowledge of her husband's occupation and then to find a way to use that information to launch a career for herself.

"Then I started doing market research interviews for Larry," said Pat.

"Besides college courses, three boys, and a home?" I asked.

Her reaction mirrored most home-based women's feelings: "I loved it. Getting out of the house. Meeting people."

Even after she graduated and worked as an elementary school substitute, Pat continued interviewing and brainstorming market research ideas with her husband. "I found the discussions fascinating, very exciting intellectually." Yet within months she had a new dilemma. She had discovered that teaching did not please her.

"Then I was lucky. At lunch one day one of Larry's business friends turned to me and said, 'You know so much about market research. Why don't you go into it? I need more help. I'll hire you.'

"As soon as he said it, I knew I could do it. Of course, I could do it! I told him, 'I will if I can run the jobs myself.'

" 'O.K.,' he said.

"And there I was in business."

Running the jobs meant receiving the market research assignment. Then it became Pat's task to bring together trained interviewers, locate suitable groups throughout the United States to interview, and supervise her interviewers to see that sampling and the project were properly done.

When I asked Pat if she thought she *could* have won a job had she been forced to look instead of having it handed to her, she nodded. "Sure. As a supervisor. Definitely. I'd been doing it, knew the jargon, techniques, formats, everything. Problem is I probably wouldn't have seen myself as qualified and might not have thought of doing it."

When I interviewed her, Pat had been in business for four years. She had taken that start and expanded her market research to a highly profitable four-day-a-week free-lance career. Preferring the freedom and time flexibility of free-lancing to a company position, she has all the business she can handle, sent to her by the many people she had met and impressed during the years she had worked for Larry. Her career involves setting up and regularly supervising crews of 12 to 40 as they research an assignment; flying to cities throughout the United States to troubleshoot for clients whose supervisors have encountered difficulties; continuing development of new research techniques; and organizing, moderating, reporting, and analyzing in-depth "focus group" market research projects.

What Have You Accidentally Learned from
Your Husband's Occupation?

The trick, as mentioned a few pages ago, is *recognition* of what you have learned.

You have not been doing "nothing" all these years. You have been talking, listening, learning. Many of the things you know about your husband's occupation may strike you as everyday "common knowledge," but it is not. It is very specialized information that you have gradually absorbed over ten, fifteen, twenty-five years. Recognize this specialized expertise whatever it is and use it to start somewhere near the middle or top of the career ladder instead of as a beginner.

It works like this: A friend of a friend of mine, is married to a man who is a public relations writer by day, a struggling short story writer by night. For fifteen years Eleanor has been hearing about, reading, and sometimes working with him on public relations releases. She has also read, discussed, and typed his stories. As long as she thought of herself as having "done nothing" while her children were young, she was rudderless. But as soon as she took these scraps of experience and listed them in impressive terms on a resume—"Ten years' experience free-lance public relations release writing for X.Y.Z. company." "Ten years' experience editing fiction"—she was able to combine this with her B.A. degree and capture a newspaper editing job with her local newspaper. "I took three days before going jobhunting and memorized the copyediting symbols. That was that." Two years ago she was promoted to editor of the newspaper's weekend magazine section.

Another woman has helped her husband, who is a commercial artist. Because she enjoys working with her hands and because it lightened her husband's load, she has become adept at lettering and paste-up work. "I don't have any formal training for anything. I couldn't imagine what I could apply for."

This mistaken obsession with "formal training" blinds millions of women to what they already know.

Samples of this woman's artwork, together with seven years of paste-up and lettering experience with her commercial artist husband, can be put together into an impressive resume. Certainly those years equal anything Ginny could have absorbed from "formal training." Yet, until she saw this, she was unable to apply for or obtain the commercial art job she was well qualified to hold.

What is it you have learned over the years while you listened to and perhaps aided your husband with his occupation? Is he in personnel work? Perhaps you have never really worked with him. Yet you have heard so much about it by now that you probably have a good grasp of interview techniques, enough knowledge to enable him to teach you in a few weeks what you need to know about standardized personnel tests. More important, stored away in your mind is all you have slowly absorbed as he discussed people problems, union problems, management problems. Why can't you put this knowledge and experience into a formal resume and invent yourself a career in personnel work?

Is your husband a self-employed accountant? During tax season, have you ever helped with the less complex forms? Could you hold a bookkeeping job. Bookkeeping, incidentally is a desperately *under*staffed occupation (see page 226 for information on jobs with favorable outlooks). If you are interested, you will quickly find a profitable niche. If you want varied days, choose a small office where one person has to handle a variety of tasks. Life will be busy and interesting. As soon as the office grows, you are the logical person to become supervisor.

Is your husband in sales? Then you are ahead of Heidi Friedman. You already know much about the world and techniques of selling. Perhaps his kind of sales has also exposed you to information about work as a buyer, creating retail floor displays, and training and supervising salespeople.

What Have You Learned Because Your Husband Did Not Know How to Do It for Himself?

Another whole world of careers may "accidentally" be open to you *because you may have developed expertise in an area of your husband's job that he did not know how to handle.* For example, a pediatrician's wife decorated and furnished three offices for him as he moved through his career. Interior decorating appeals to many women, but few are able to make a paying occupation of it.

This doctor's wife had taste and flair. Without in any way creating a "cutesy" look, she chose the bright colors, the shapes, designs, and accessories that made each of her husband's offices uniquely suited to a pediatrician's patients, yet attractive and serene enough for parents. When friends commented on her work, she had the insight to realize that here was a potential business. Because her husband was unable to decorate his offices, she practiced on him and went on to a very interesting and specialized career decorating medical and dental offices.

Two other women, wives of corporate executives, have built very lucrative careers by learning a business *while helping their husbands through tasks the men could not handle.* Both women were very active in local amateur dramatic groups. When their husbands admitted they suffered miserably if they had to deliver a speech, be interviewed, or otherwise meet the public, the wives coached them. When the men mentioned that almost every executive they knew went through similar agonies, *the women recognized the expertise they had to offer.* They enrolled at a nearby college for some formal communication courses, collected speech, drama, and communications texts, and from them developed exercises and teaching ideas.

With these materials they created a "seminar package," ran it first at their husbands' businesses, then at businesses of their husbands' friends. Now, experienced and confident, for $600 a day they visit a corporation, take a tiny group of executives, and conduct seminars on how to behave while being interviewed, how to prepare and deliver a speech, and how to present an idea or proposal at a meeting. They have more business than they are willing to undertake. Lately they have solved that by selling their first franchise. During a European vacation, one of the partners made the arrangement with another member of her tourist group, a dynamic woman from California. By trip's end, the woman had paid the partners $5,000 for the package information and was on her way home to arrange her own seminars.

How to Think Through to Your Own Expertise

Ask yourself the following questions: (1) What have I done to help my husband with his job? (2) What have I learned about his occupation simply from listening and talking to him about it all these years? When you have the answers to 1 and 2, make up a resume that reflects that knowledge in impressive business terms. Then go out and capture an interesting middle- or upper-echelon job or career in that field. Other possible questions are (3) What have I done to help my husband with his work because I was better at it (decorating, making a speech, editing) than he was? and (4) Are there many people who could use the same help? If the answer to 4 is yes, you now have the focus of a great job or career.

What Was Your Biggest Shock?

As I ended my interview with Pat, I asked her to tell me the most important thing she had learned since beginning her career. Allowing for mood changes, she felt, was something most women might have to adjust to. One week you're riding high, and everything is going well. The next week, someone calls you down on something, "and you're frantically ready to believe you're incompetent. You have to learn that all that's happened is you've made a mistake. Everyone—including the people who are chewing you out—makes mistakes. Of course, if you don't learn from your mistakes, then . . ."

I asked her if there was one thing that stood out in her mind as the biggest shock she had while making the transition from home to career. She smiled. "I'm still not used to being complimented for a job I've done," she said. "I really knock myself out in my work, throw myself into it one hundred percent; yet it's always a surprise to me when a client tells me, 'Good job, Pat.' When a woman is home for many years with her housework and children, she often ends up believing she can't function or compete in the business world. Even when you succeed, as I have, it takes a long time to get over the surprise."

SECTION IV

GREAT TWO- TO SIX-HOUR-A-WEEK JOBS

1
You Already Have
All the Qualifications

For the woman who is still very occupied with young children, or for the woman who enjoys her home-centered life but would like "just a few hours of interesting paid work a week," this section can provide the ideal great job or career.

This book discusses both part-time and full-time job and career ideas. However, the part-time jobs discussed in all the other sections usually require at least two to three mornings, afternoons, or evenings a week of your time—that is, portions of a few *days* weekly.

The part-time jobs in this section are different. They are so undemanding and their requirements for time are so flexible that as little as two *hours* employment weekly can give you an exciting, prestigious and (per hour) very remunerative job. Also, whereas all other part-time jobs must be individually developed by you and your employer, the short-hour jobs in this section already exist in huge supply. They are out there waiting for you.

Should your free time grow or your appetite for a career increase, *you can expand your original few hours weekly as much as you wish.* Chapter 2 of this section tells how.

In the search for fulfilling and significant part-time work, most women face fewer obstacles than Carole Arund did. The basic solution Carole eventually discovered suggests *a career approach almost any woman could use. Though Carole's own career revolves around music, her solution has nothing to do with music, itself. Music just happens to be the field in which Carole applies her insights. To use Carole's method to create a career for yourself, no college study is necessary, though the work would certainly challenge and satisfy a college graduate.*

"I had some special problems," says Carole Arund, "because at age twenty I had three babies within eleven months. First my husband and I had a son, and then eleven months later girl twins. All I could do was just about survive those infant-toddler years. It was like having triplets. My husband did the best he could to help but he was struggling to support us all and at the same time attend college."

As Carole and I sat together in her airy suburban living room dominated by a piano and a very personal collection of nostalgia and flea market antiques, it was hard to visualize Carole as ever having been discouraged. "But, oh, I was so young and it was very hard." Stress, combined with a thyroid deficiency that mystified doctor after doctor, brought Carole's weight to over 200 pounds and produced a tormenting skin ailment. Through her college years, which began when the twins were three years old, she dieted off 60 pounds and, with thyroid treatment conquered the skin ailment. Then capitalizing on her 5 feet 7 inches of height and a flair for offbeat, interesting clothes, she developed into a striking woman.

After seven years of struggling part-time through college, Carole emerged, six months before her thirtieth birthday, with a bachelor's degree and teaching certificate, only to confront the problem of what to do with them. Echoing a dilemma many women face, Carole explains, "I started college and completed most of it without knowing what career I expected college to provide me with. I couldn't figure it out. When I became a fine arts major, I don't know exactly what I thought I'd do with it."

A course in techniques of teaching music to children, taken during her senior year, "opened a world of ideas for me on how very young children could be led through music, dance, and song to grow and develop into healthier, happier people. I decided that was what I wanted to do."

But I Couldn't Work Full-Time

Like many women with young children, Carole couldn't accept a full-time job. Teaching music in a school is an unusually exhausting job, different from normal classroom teaching. The music teacher takes a whole school every day, a period at a time in each class, working at top speed every minute. "I'd have been too tired for my own family. My children were eight and nine then. Giving lessons after school was no solution. That's when my own children were home needing me."

In reading magazines and newspaper interviews with people who managed to find fulfilling work, Carole had noticed that these people often discovered their opportunities in everyday life. They constantly seemed to apply the question, "How can I use my skill here?" to different situations they met each day. Starting with this outlook, Carole began tearing items from newspapers and magazines or jotting down job opportunities from supermarket bulletin boards. "I didn't know exactly what I was looking for—just a lead of some kind."

At the town Fourth of July parade, Carole's open, questing attitude produced results. A float called "Saturday School" from the neighboring town of Princevale suggested that Princevale planned special classes and culture on Saturday for schoolchildren.

Early the next morning Carole began phoning friends, acquaintances, and town officials until she learned enough about "Saturday School" to be intelligent about it. Then, and only then, did she dial the Saturday School office. Asking for the director (the higher the administrator you talk to in any situation, the more power she or he has to act, and the better your chances of success are), Carole explained her qualifications and asked, "Wouldn't you want to offer a music program for very young children also?" Because of her need to be home on weekends with her own youngsters, she offered the program for preschool children and kindergartens one morning a week, thereby inventing the preschool music course for them and, moreover, for a time *that would fit her own life.*

The idea was accepted. The town charged parents $20, or $2 a lesson for each 10-week session. Carole was paid $10 an hour.

Adult Education and Recreation Programs

Once she stumbled on this idea, Carole realized that the approach of selling her skill part-time to a town's community or adult school (run by the board of education, recreation or parks commission, library, or museum) *was applicable to every town in her area.* (Carole's course was for child education, but the vast majority of the educational and recreational programs offered by community schools are for *adults* and are given both during the day and evening.) Carole tested her idea of selling her talents to several communities by calling the program director of her own town and asking for an interview. As in many towns, some of their courses were free to citizens, and the teacher was paid by the town. For other courses, registrants were asked to pay, and the tuition collected was passed to the teacher. This was the plan her town suggested to Carole. Thus, a session of 12 children at the same $2 a session could yield Carole $24 an hour.

Within the last 25 years, town-supported courses in adult schools, recreational programs, or extension schools (by whatever name) have become an established nationwide phenomenon. Charles Wood, Executive Director of the Adult Education Association of the United States of America in an interview with me, estimated that more than 90 percent of all American communities offer basic educational skill programs and 80 percent offer widely varied adult programs. He stressed that 80 percent is the association's best "estimate."

Cities, he said, may offer thousands of adult courses, when the various board of education, recreation commission, library, and museum courses are counted. And many *small* suburban towns may offer as many as *200 to 300. Often, the number of courses provided depends on what citizens can teach. On pages 105 to 113 we list 264 typical courses that are currently available in towns in the United States.* There you will find courses in nearly everything, including crafts, sports, languages, practical skills, culture, lifestyle, enrichment, and fun courses.

But I Don't Know Anything That Well

Before you draw back and say, "But I don't know anything well enough to teach it," wait till you read the course lists. You will probably discover more than one course that you could teach. *In addition, if you wish, teaching at a community school can be only a beginning, a platform from which to launch several part-time careers.* (A chapter on "Potential for Expanding Your Two- to Six-Hour Great Job follows.)

With increased leisure, longer lives, and hunger for participation in life rather than spectator living, young people and adults are anxious to develop new interests and skills. Even poor economic conditions and job worries do not affect enrollment in adult courses. During the 1975–1976 recession, enrollment continued to soar.

If you are interested enough in a subject to have become good at it, chances are there are other people in your area who would be interested in learning about it. Prove it to yourself by reading the list at the end of this section. Would you ever have guessed that there were students for some of these topics?

Your town and your neighboring towns may call their programs by various names. If you want to learn what is available in your area, begin by calling the board of education, town recreation or parks commission, public library, or museum. And remember should a community *not* offer anything like your subject, your opportunity will be all the greater.

Even if your course already exists, you may be able to offer a variation. For example, even if Typing for Beginners is already listed in your town's catalogue, perhaps you can teach Typing Refresher, Intermediate Typing, Clerical Practice, or Key Punch. If you have had dance training or experience, you may find one or more dance courses already listed, but perhaps you could offer Ballroom Dancing, Ballet, Modern Dance, or Choreography for Amateur and Semiprofessional Theater. If the basic crafts and culture topics are already spoken for by other teachers, perhaps you could handle Oil Painting, Woodworking, Knitting, Sculpture, Basic Drawing, Stitchery, Wallhangings and Rug Making, Batik and Tie Dye, Package Design, Cake Decorating, Beginning

Wine Making, Leaded Stained Glass, Barbershop Quartet and Chorus Singing, Group Piano, Needlepoint, Off-Loom Weaving, Quilting, Tailoring, Sewing with Knits, Slipcovers and Draperies, Crocheting, Great Books, Great European Portrait Painters, Camping, Backpacking, Hiking, Modern English Poetry, Remedial Tennis, Doubles Tennis, Public Speaking, Bookkeeping, Accounting.

In addition to teaching, your search for a variation of a course *may give you the opportunity to demonstrate and sharpen your executive and managerial skills.* Instead of teaching tennis, bridge, Mah-Jongg, chess, and other games, could you propose a tournament course for people who are already accomplished players? For your tournament course, you could organize your sessions into a round-robin that would produce a town champion at the end of the course. At the same time you could win public attention and excitement for your program by visiting local businesses and getting them to donate championship prizes and then seeing to it that your tournament, the prize donors and winners, and, of course, you receive appropriate publicity in your town paper.

If your town is one of the relatively few that has no adult program, you could suggest it to the board of education. Decide what course you would like to offer, and visit the head of the board of education or the appropriate official. You will probably find it simple and easy to take the direct approach, suggest your course, make the arrangements, and go ahead. However, if you want official backing, Charles Wood suggests you write or call the dean of extension of your state's land-grant college. If you do not know its name, your library can tell you. The office of the dean of extension is often eager to bring you together with the appropriate community official and thereby lend an official status to your effort.

The lists at the end of this section are drawn from real courses offered by American communities. They are only a beginning, meant to provide a mental springboard.

Some of the course catalogues of adult schools actually spell out an invitation for teachers, "TEACHERS WANTED!!!," all caps and three exclamation points. Other catalogues imply a relaxed, open-door invitation to teachers. The intriguing, erratic mixture of courses available in various towns telegraphs the message, "We'll take just about anybody who knows something and wants to teach. Just get in touch with us."

Sometimes a course is so popular that a community uses two, three, or more teachers for the subject. *This means that even though you see your potential course in a town's catalogue, you may find that they are anxious to employ another teacher for that subject.* Inquire.

No course that you can develop is so humble that it cannot grow into an exciting career or business that will yield you prestige, the pleasure of accomplishment, and profit. One woman in our town has built an entire career around her love of dogs. She began teaching dog obedience classes at the town's adult school only one session a week, which meant minimal financial return. Within two years, through the teaching of this one course, word of her ability has spread through the area. The barrage of requests for private dog training and show handling has given her excellent income and complete independence to make her own hours. At present she schedules and visits "clients" for obedience training five mornings a week, from ten to one o'clock. "That gives me a standing as an 'expert,' something to do daily that I really enjoy, plenty of time to myself and for my family, and twelve dollars an hour. Well, that's one hundred eighty dollars a week for fifteen hours interesting work."

2
Potential for Expanding
Your Two- to Six-Hour
Great Job

Publicity

In addition to the immediate gratification of a job and income, you can use your town teaching in numerous ways. Once you have the advantage of this kind of exposure, you will have become a "star" in your subject, a leader in your area in a specific skill. It is important, Carole has learned, to call your local newspaper, tell them about you course, and ask if they would like to do a story about it. Usually they are glad to bring an account of anything new to the community. Within the last ten years, American suburbia has been blanketed by an explosion of local weekly or semiweekly tabloid-size newspapers, often called "shoppers," which are supported by supermarket and other advertisements and are distributed free throughout the community. Everyone in town receives a copy, and everyone falls into the habit of reading it. Though the major city newspaper in your area may be disinterested in your story, the local is usually skimpily staffed and will seize upon and allow your feature news space and perhaps even pictorial coverage.

Better even than calling the newspaper is writing an account on the course yourself and bringing it into the paper's office. The staff may be too busy to act on your phone conversation or may write the story inaccurately.

There is nothing "pushy" or ostentatious about such action. You are in business now, the business of teaching your subject, and all businesses thrive on publicity. The publicity of a feature story (which, of course, costs you nothing) in your local paper *will help you now as it informs potential students of the existence of your course. Later clippings of that publicity will be immensely useful in selling another town or another potential employer on your course.*

Word of mouth, your telling others what you have done, often is difficult for people to evaluate. An article in a newspaper about your work, however, has enormous impact on most people, even those who are sophisticated and worldly. It may not be logical, but it is true. The prestigious scientific publication *Journal of Social Psychology* confirmed this observation in a research study report, "The Power of the Printed Word." The psychologists tested the hypothesis that "the mere fact that a communication is printed gives it an aura of significance, importance, and value" and found it to be true!

In everyday life, this research means that your course will be boosted because people's common reaction to your article in the newspaper will be, "It must be important. It must be a success."

If your course is visual, as Carole's is—the children can be seen dancing and creating to the music—explain this to your newspaper and ask if they would like to send a photographer. Or even better, when you bring your article about the course, include a candid of the group to indicate the picture potential to the editor. It is easier for an editor, seeing the picture, to recognize the potential of the story and accept it. In your sample candid, you should, of course, have the group doing something. Snap them engaged in their activity, not staring stiffly into the camera.

No matter what the topic of your course, there is usually no need to worry about pupils. The supply of interested students constantly renews itself. Though my mother volunteered her services, her 20 years of experience teaching Braille to normal-sighted people who wanted to learn to transcribe books for the blind are a good example of the general rule. The town where my mother lived was relatively small, and year after year she thought she had surely exhausted the supply of interested pupils. Each June, when the course concluded, she featured the names of her "graduates" in an article for the various local newspapers, together with an announcement of enrollment for the next year's class. Each September there was a fresh group of 10 to 15 eager men and women. The explanation is simple and would apply to your courses also.

Year by year, people move into different stages of their lives. Whereas last year they might not have been interested in learning Braille, or whatever you teach, this year their children may have reached kindergarten age, or the children may be away at college, and they have time; or they may have decided to cultivate a new hobby or skill, and they make time; or they may have retired from their job and have time; or they may find themselves at home with a new baby, and your course may be what they are searching for to take them outside the house. Next year another batch of people will have moved into a stage of life with interests and needs that your course will suit.

Career Opportunities from Town Teaching

You may find that teaching one or two courses in your own and neighboring towns is exactly what you want your part-time career to be. If, however, you want to expand your teaching of your skill or hobby, your town teaching work can be a strong credential. Community colleges across the country now offer numerous noncredit or "life" courses and seminars—everything from Chess and Backgammon Seminars to New Patterns in Marriage to Real Estate License Preparation. For these courses you need skill in the subject rather than a formal college education and you are paid at the prevailing rate of the college. If your skill is in an intellectual subject and you do have sufficient college background of your own, you may be able to offer yourself as an adjunct (part-time) instructor for one or more courses that do carry college credit.

Investigate the community services, extension schools, Saturday colleges, and other special programs your nearby two-year and four-year colleges offer. Many academic institutions have responded to the post-1973 drop in teen-age student applications by opening or adding to their community, women's or extension divisions. Reaching out to another kind of student body is a very popular current educational concept. With these divisions and the courses they offer lie the colleges' hopes for solvency.

Consequently, you will find that if your course can attract enough students to pay your salary and earn something for the college, your offer to teach will usually be greeted with warmth and interest. If your course is already drawing well at your town school, there is your prima facie proof of the value of your program. Since you are already a professional teacher of the subject, the college may feel you are experienced enough and well qualified to teach the course for them.

Depending on your subject, college degrees may or may not be necessary. A man I know who has 20 years of experience as a salesman teaches a class in sales at a community college, though he has no master's degree. According to state law, to teach as part of the permanent staff of a community college a teacher *must* hold a master's degree or better. But different standards apply to teaching part-time: in this man's case, his practical experience as a salesman was deemed the equivalent of the master's, and he landed the job. A woman who had completed only 1 year of college about 25 years ago also teaches at a community college. Her subject is magazine article writing. The college considers the woman's accomplishments as a published writer as sufficient credentials. Another woman, in Rockland County, New York, "found herself" in weaving. Her job teaching weaving at a community school led to a community college weaving course and eventually to an offer from an investor to join him in opening a crafts store. He would supply the money; she, the knowledge and talent. Another woman, in her twenties, still deeply involved in caring for her toddler and baby keeps her skills bright by taking time off from her baby tending to teach one course a week at a four-year state college. How did she get it? She applied, told them what her field of study had been, and was hired.

In addition to colleges, nearby shopping centers may also be sources of money and glamorous teaching assignments. Every good-sized shopping center has a public relations director whose daily job requires him or her to place news—not bought ads— about the shopping center into local newspapers. For example, a feature in your local paper about some sports or entertainment star who will "visit" your shopping center has been placed by the public relations director, and that star has, of course, been hired. You have probably also read items about other events, or "promotions," as they are often called, to be held at your shopping center: for example Beautiful Baby Contest or a Crafts

Sale Day sponsored by the churches, synagogues, and women's clubs of your area, or a free Beach Fashion Show. These, too, have been planned and then publicized by the hard-pressed public relations director. The purpose, naturally, is to acquire free newspaper space through stories about the shopping center. The ultimate hope and purpose are to cause you, the reader, to say to yourself, "I think I'll go to that." Once you are at the center for the event, the public relations department will have succeeded if you decide, "While I'm here, I'll buy a few things I've been needing."

Public relations directors search constantly for new ideas for promotions. One huge shopping center has held free carpentry and plumbing classes. Another major store offered a class in Playwrights of the 20th Century. Cooking classes and craft classes appear regularly in meeting halls of shopping centers. Once you have your course established, develop a variation of it and offer it to the public relations director as a shopping center promotion. Each person can pay a small fee at the door, from which you will collect your payment, or the shopping center may be willing to hand you a flat amount and feel itself rewarded when you draw a good group of potential shoppers to your meetings.

What would be a variation of your present course? Perhaps you teach a foreign language. Just before the vacation season, the shopping center could offer a four-session French for Tourists. Wouldn't it be logical to believe that after your tourist lessons, the travelers-to-be would shop for their vacation clothes at that center? Do you teach photography? How about a four-session How to Take Great Pictures on Your Vacation for the same summer or winter vacationers-to-be? Now you would have a course that would attract potential customers of both clothes and cameras. Do you teach some kind of art? Perhaps a How to Enjoy the Great Art, Buildings, and Churches You See Abroad for the same tourists.

As the Playwrights of the 20th Century course indicates, not every course has to have heavy practical application. The playwrights course was of value to the store because through it the store hoped to attract an educated, sophisticated group who would appreciate and buy in its couture collection located immediately next to the lecture room.

Do not depend on the busy public relations personnel to see the possible appeal of your program. You should be prepared to explain the potential customer attractions for any course you wish to teach.

If your course would benefit a particular store in that shopping center or a particular section of a department store, perhaps you could encourage the manager of that section to approach the center's public relations director on your behalf. A typing course given during late August and early September, when the back-to-school and back-to-college shopping rush is at its height, might be extremely attractive to either the teen clothing departments or to the typewriter and school-supplies department of a large store. A course in Natural Childbirth Exercises for prospective mothers might be very appealing to a store in the center selling baby's wear, toys, equipment, and furniture. Your Camera Tips for Vacationers should sound exciting to the camera mart. Once managers understand that your course would bring into the center students who are potential customers for their specialty, they are certain to be interested in seeing that the center sponsors your lessons. They will help you sell the public relations director.

Does the craft shop in your area give lessons or demonstrations? Why not? Perhaps they don't have a teacher. Maybe they, too, could use a part-time teacher with your specialty.

If you decide that your teaching should be a stepping stone to something else, as a town-teacher expert on the subject, you will regularly be in contact with people interested in your ability. Word of your skill will spread through the publicity that you will receive when the town itself publicizes the program and when you encourage local newspapers to cover your course. If you respond to those you meet with Carole's question in mind, "How can I find another situation to use my ability?" you will be in an ideal position to gather information and expand your career.

3
How Exactly Would You Sell Your Idea?

Applying These Techniques for Selling Your Idea Exactly to You

Says Carole Arund, "In selling my idea for my Music Time course to different towns and failing to sell it in other towns, I've learned how to help insure your success. In getting the first job at Saturday School, with beginner's luck I did things right. Later, when I sometimes failed, I looked back and recognized what was needed."

Preliminary Self-Briefing: As we mentioned in Chapter 1 of this section, before speaking to the Saturday School director, Carole called people till she had enough information about the program and how it expected to work, so she could think through her idea and then explain it *in a way that would fit into their format.*

Payment: Carole had to prepare in her mind various ways of receiving income: (1) The town could pay her directly; (2) the town could collect registration fees from participants and divide fees with her; or (3) the town could collect registration fees, turning over all to her. For example, when Carole's ideas were in danger of being rejected in her home town ("We're sorry. We like your idea but we don't have anything in the budget to pay a teacher for this."), she was able to suggest that hers be a fee course, which would provide her pay. Then her course was accepted.

Attracting Students: Though the recreation commission of her town listed Carole's course with all the others, she felt that, as the teacher, "I couldn't depend on just that. Because the board of education sponsored the course, all participants had to be kindergarten school age; younger children couldn't have been covered by the town insurance."

The day before school opened that September, when she knew teachers would be setting up their classrooms, Carole visited all eight kindergarten teachers in town. Introducing herself, she explained what the program tried to accomplish for children. By doing this, she felt that when parents of the kindergarteners asked the teacher, "Do you know whether this program is worthwhile?" the teachers would know something about it and might consider recommending it.

In attracting students for your class you could discover the proper people to contact simply by asking yourself, "Who are the potential students for my course?" "Where do they congregate?" "What organizations (such as the library, women's clubs, Rotary, Junior Chamber of Commerce, religious groups) do they now belong to where I could reach a number of them at a time and thus encourage word-of-mouth publicity about my course?"

When you have the answers to those questions, you set about reaching those groups. Write a personal note to the presidents of the organizations, enclosing a notice of your course and suggesting that members may find it pleasant and interesting. Offer to come to a meeting of the organization as a free speaker or demonstrator to give a short preview session as part of their entertainment program. Distribute signs on library, supermarket, and other bulletin boards. And, of course, provide your local newspaper with an article and picture.

Convincing the People in Charge: In a town where Carole failed to sell her course, the 17-member board of recreational commissioners held the power. "At that point I was so busy with other projects, I didn't do the necessary preliminary 'convincing' work," Carole explains. *"Laying the groundwork beforehand is what any woman who wants to teach any course should think about.*

"Where authorities have to vote on it," Carole says, "as with my seventeen commissioners, I should have seen to it that they knew about the course before they arrived to vote and that they had a chance to understand what it was. To do this, I could have taken a photocopy of a newspaper article that told about the course's value to another town and mailed the photocopy with a

short explanation note before the meeting to each official, saying
that this is what was to be proposed for their town. Then, with an
understanding of what the course could accomplish, they probably would have voted yes."

If this is your first course and you do not have a newspaper
article, Carole believes you can succeed simply by writing a note
anyway, telling what the course is and your qualifications to teach
it. Then, be at the meeting early, pleasantly greet the officials as
they arrive, and ask if there are any questions about your course.

Working from Your Own Home: Since Carole does not conduct
her Music Time class for her .new home town, she is free to use
the recreation room of her house to hold the course privately. To
publicize the course, she has again used techniques that any
woman can employ to attract students for any home course.
Carole cautions, however, that, to begin with, it is usually far
better to teach for a town agency, college, or shopping center.
These institutions continually generate publicity for themselves,
and your course will profit from a listing in their catalogues, their
mail notices, their newspaper ads, and newspaper feature stories.
When you offer the course yourself, you alone have to attract all
the students. However, it can be done. Carole attracts students for
her home studio sessions of Music Time by:

1. Signs in supermarkets
2. Ads in church and synagogue newsletters
3. A big newspaper article that has been written about her
   course and turned into a mimeographed flyer, which her
   children tuck into neighborhood mailboxes
4. Direct phone calls to people suggested by her friends
5. And, again, best of all, the interest and excitement
   generated by getting a local paper to write a new story
   about the course. For this, a story about each "graduating
   class" is a useful perennial idea since local papers value
   local names. Then another story later on, entitled "Registration Is Open."

Overall, by following Carole Arund's system of building on the
hobby, skill, knowledge, or interest you have been developing
during your full-time homemaker years, you can create part-time
paid activities and courses that will bring many rewards: a job

that exercises both your teaching and leadership skills; contact with people; and a chance to display your knowledge, which in turn can lead you to numerous other part-time and full-time job opportunities.

Following are 264 courses, *samples taken from current catalogues.* (Occasionally, where the course title is enigmatic, I'll add the description from the catalogue.)

Arts & Crafts

Arts and Crafts to Teach to Children
Bonsai
Calligraphy
Candle Making for Fun and Profit: Basic, Advanced
Ceramics
Clay
Crafts à la Carte (a potpourri of crafts, paper, tole, découpage
        under glass, tinsel painting, painting on plaster, and
        so on)
Colonial Crafts
Creative Satin Flower Design
Dried Natural Materials: Where to Gather, How to Arrange
Holiday Decorations
Jewelry Making
Leathercraft
Metalworking
Pottery
Pysanky (Ukranian Easter eggs decoration)
Silversmithing
Stained Glass Art
Terrariums, Dish-Gardens
Tie Dying and Batik
Woodworking: Beginners, General

Business Skills and Careers

Accounting: Basic, Advanced
Advertising
Aviation: Instrument Pilot Ground School
Aviation: Private and Commercial Pilot Ground School
Blueprint Reading

Bookkeeping: Basic, Intermediate, Advanced
Business English and Communication
Business Math
Careers for Women (ideas for housewives interested in entering
      the job market)
Clerical Practice
College Algebra
Computing: Introduction
Electronics: Basic
Fortran Programming
Home Management
Home Nursing
Income Tax
Instrument Rating School
Interior Decorating
Investments
Law: For the Layman
Law Theories
Office Practice
Operations Management
Power Plant: Black Seal License, Advanced Seal License
Principles of Supervision: Beginners, Advanced
Probability and Statistics: Introduction
Real Estate: Broker's Course
Real Estate: Salesman's Course
Refrigeration: Introduction
Secretarial Producedures
Shorthand: Refresher
Stenography: Beginners, Advanced
Stenography: Gregg
Stenoscript (ABC shorthand)
Stock Market: Beginners, Advanced
Substitute Teaching
Survey of Retail Store Operations
Tools for Increasing Profits for the Small Business Owner
Travel Agency Course
Typing: Elementary, Intermediate
Typing: Refresher
Typing, Electric: Advanced
Typing, Memory: Advanced

Creative Arts

English Composition
Journalism
Photography:
  Introduction, B & W and Color
  Advanced, Including Darkroom
  Color Slides
  Concept and Techniques
  Landscape and Design
  Portrait
  Workshop
Radio Broadcasting: Introduction
Science of Creative Intelligence
Writing Workshop, Creative: Beginners, Intermediate

Culinary Arts

Adventures in Middle East Cooking
Basic Cooking
Cake Decorating
Chinese Cooking
Cooking for Two
French Gourmet Cooking
Herbalism
Japanese Cooking
The Return of Home Baking
Vegetarian Cooking
Wine Tasting and Wine Appreciation

Dance

Ballroom Dancing
Belly Dancing
Exotic: Beginners
Folk
Greek Dancing
Modern Dance and Creative Movement for Children
Modern Dance for Teen-agers
Rhythmic Jazz

Social Dancing, Part I: American
Social Dancing, Part II: Latin

Drama

An Approach to Acting
Shakespeare's Plays
Shakespeare's Plays: His Notion of Children
Theater Appreciation
Theater: Farce and Comedy in It
Voice and Drama

Fix It

Antique Clock Repair
Antique Restoration and Caning
Automobile Maintenance
Care and Maintenance of Home Swimming Pools
Furniture Refinishing
Hi-Fi and You Fix It
Home Improvement Projects
Home Repair
Upholstery
Welding Fundamentals
Women Under the Car Hood
Your Ten-Speed Bike Repairs

Hobbies

Astrology: Beginners, Intermediate, Advanced
Collectibles: Nostalgia
Graphology: The Psychology of Writing
Numerology
Palmistry
Stamp Collecting
Understanding the Home Garden

Language

French: Beginners, Intermediate, Advanced
German: Beginners, Intermediate

Hebrew: Beginners, Intermediate
Hieroglyphics (Egyptian)
Italian: Beginners, Intermediate
Language and Thinking
Languages, Conversational Approach:
  Chinese
  Dutch
  French
  German
  Japanese
  Norwegian
Spanish: Beginners, Intermediate, Advanced Conversational

Literature

Black Literature
Modern American Dramatists
Poetry as Therapy
Romantic English Poets
Salvation and Damnation
Self-Awareness in Poetry
Sex as a Motif in Modern Novels
Women in English Novels

Living Skills

Advances in Parapsychology
Alternatives for Living: Farming, Getting Back to the Land
College Board SAT: Algebra Review
  English Preparation
  Geometry Review
Consciousness Raising for Men and Women
Consumer Frauds
Dale Carnegie Course
Dilemmas of Contemporary Adult Living
Driver Education
Female in Contemporary Adult Living
General Psychology
Hair Care and Face Make-up
High School Equivalency: I, II

Improve Your Grades
Lip Reading
Male in Contemporary Society
Meditation for Self-Improvement
Memory and Concentration
Memory Improvement Seminar
Men's Lib and Bachelor's Survival (sewing and cooking)
Metric System: All You Need to Know
Mind Control
Modern Mathematics: Introduction
New Image
New Math for Parents
Personality Development and Interaction
Preparation for Retirement Seminar
Psychology of Interpersonal Relations
Public Speaking
Speak Up and Sell Your Idea
Speed Reading
Taking the Mystery Out of Insurance
Transcendental Meditation
Your Voice, Your Speech: Use Them Effectively

Martial Arts

Judo, Karate, Jujitsu Techniques
Karate: Self-Defense
   For Teenagers
   For Women
Kung-fu

Music

Bagpipe Playing
Banjo: I, II
Choral Seminar
Guitar: Children, 8–14
Guitar: Finger Picking
Guitar, for Adults: Beginners, Intermediate
Listening to Classical Music
Music Appreciation

Music for the Handicapped
Organ Playing for Beginners
Organ Playing: II, III, IV
Piano: for Pleasure
Piano: for Beginners
Piano: II, III, IV

Needlecraft and Sewing

Bargello (a form of needlepoint)
Crewel Embroidery
Crocheting
Knitting
Knitting: Advanced
Macramé
Needlepoint
Needlepoint: Design Your Own
Needlepoint: For Men
Patchwork Quilts
Rug Hooking and Rug Braiding
Sewing: Beginners, Intermediate, Advanced
Sewing: Creative
Sewing: Draperies, Bedspreads, Tablecloths
Sewing: Infants and Children
Sewing with Knits
Tailoring: Men and Women
Weaving

Painting and Sculpture

Art Made Simple (for people without any art background)
Chinese Brush Painting
Decorative Tole Painting
Drawing: Elementary
Great Artists
Language of Art
Life Drawing
Painting: Acrylics
Painting: Oil
Sculpting: Beginners, Advanced

Understanding Art Before You Buy a Painting
Watercolor and Pencil Sketching

Pets

Canine Husbandry
Dog Grooming
Dog Obedience
Horse Grooming
Poodle Grooming

Physical Fitness

Diet Control
Hatha Yoga
Health Spa Slimnastics
Nutrition: A Unified Approach to Life Studies
Physical Conditioning for Men
Recreational Education for the Handicapped
Smokenders, N.J., Inc.
Tiny Tots' Gym
Weight Control
Why Risk a Heart Attack?
Women's Physical Fitness
Yoga

Science

Acoustics and Noise Control: Basic
Anatomy and Physiology for the Layman
Earth Science for the Layman

Sports

Baton Twirling
Boating: Basic
Bowling Instructions: Beginners, Advanced
Golf: Beginners
Hiking in Local Area
Horseback Riding: Beginners, Intermediate, Advanced
Ice Skating

Junior Boatman Techniques
Local Bicycle Trips
Ski, Learn to
Skiing: She and Ski
Sports Night for Women
Tennis: Student, Adult, Clinic, Doubles
Volleyball for Women
Wilderness Backpacking

Table Games

Backgammon
Bridge, Contract: Beginners, Intermediate, Advanced, Tournament
Chess for Fun: Beginners, Intermediate, Advanced, Tournament
Table Tennis

Miscellaneous

Citizenship for New Americans: Basic, Advanced
Electric Energy Production and the Environment
English as a Second Language
English for New Americans: Beginners, Advanced
First Aid: Standard Course
   Red Cross
   Advanced and Emergency Care
Medical Aide Training
Police: Their Scope and Responsibility Within the Community
Preserving Nature's Treasures
Rebels and Redcoats (American history)
Travel, the Joy of
Women: A Second Career

And remember, these are only *samples* of courses currently being offered.

SECTION V:

LAUNCHING A CAREER IN POLITICS

1
Much Easier
Than You Might Think

Open to All Women

Getting yourself a career in politics can be much easier than you
might think. For most people, women and men, politics sounds
complex and impenetrable. "It's not for me. How in the world
could I ever get started?" is the usual reaction of most homemakers. "Why would any political organization let me in?"

Yet any woman who exhibits an interest in her town's local
politics can probably be appointed or elected to a commission,
board, or public office," said Joan Masel, councilwoman, housewife, and mother, as she and I settled in her living room for a
detailed interview. "You need an outgoing temperament; you
have to be the kind of person who enjoys being with people and
talking to people. After that, it's simply a matter of going ahead
and getting into politics."

A full-figured, attractive woman in her early forties, Joan Masel
is councilwoman for a town of 30,000 people, with a budget of
over 16 million dollars annually. If you had to describe her in one
phrase, you might call her a very likable, very forceful woman. As
a past member of the planning board and assistance board of the
town and now as councilwoman, Joan Masel has enjoyed a
prerogative few women in our society have: power. "Like anyone
actively involved in a town's government, I'm constantly making
major decisions on policy, laws, and millions of dollars in
expenditures. I'm working in what in business would be a high
executive level."

For homemakers, a job or career in politics can offer exciting, meaningful work, a chance to put ideals and aspirations into effect, power, and continual contacts with people. The pay can vary from ample to nothing for various town, county, and state boards and commissions. Joan's council position pays $1,500 a year (many towns pay less; some pay more). Various other town and county elective and appointive political jobs yield incomes of $5,000, $10,000, $20,000, and up. Most are not full-time activities.

Joyce Ferguson, mayor of West Memphis, Arkansas (population 28,000), earns $5,000 in her job as the city's first woman mayor overseeing an all-male council. She defeated six men in this, her first, race for public office. It was past involvement in many civic projects, says Mayor Ferguson, that led to her interest in politics and her desire to "do the most for my city. . . . It's not whether you're a man or a woman. It's whether you can do the job."

Eleanor Kieliszek, the successful mayor of Teaneck, New Jersey (population 42,000), one of the few cities in the United States where racial integration has worked outstandingly well, phrases it differently. When she was sworn in as mayor, Eleanor Kieliszek's highest academic degree was her high school diploma. "Politics," says she, "is the only career where there are no degree requirements. It's like marriage."

Using Your Years of Volunteer Organization Work as a Base for a Political Career

For the millions of American women in their thirties, forties, and fifties who have gone as far as they can or wish to go with volunteer organization work, politics can be the next logical step. *Most women do not recognize how they can use their years of this kind of experience to propel themselves into a political career.* "I don't think I understood it myself when it was happening," says Joan Masel. "But, in looking back, now I see. And the same approach could be used by any interested woman."

As Joan analyzes it, "Politics, basically, as most people realize, is a popularity contest. How many votes can you draw? Any woman who has been active in an organization in town is in a position of strength to enter and succeed in local politics. Perhaps she's been a major officer of the women's group of her church or synagogue, or a leader in League of Women Voters, or Little League Mothers, or Little Theater, or any group.

"In a big city like New York or Atlanta or Seattle, of course, it's much harder. But in suburbia, where the mass of American women now live, being a leader in a town group means that you have what the politicians in town will recognize as a 'built-in constituency.' They'll feel that because the people in your organization have already demonstrated their faith in you by giving you a position of prominence, these people and their husbands and friends, too, will have faith in you and will vote for you if you become active politically. Since you can command votes, they'll automatically treat you with respect and interest."

Jeane J. Kirkpatrick, professor of government at Georgetown University, confirms Joan Masel's observation about the value of volunteer work to your political career. In *Political Woman* (New York: Basic Books, 1974) Dr. Kirkpatrick reports on a major research project she conducted into the lives of present-day female politicians. Almost without exception, the women had been energetic volunteers in all kinds of health, religious, community, and other organizations before running for political office.

> Volunteer community service provides women without specific professional or educational training for a legislative career an opportunity to acquire experience, skills, and reputations that qualify them for public office. This aspect of volunteer work is frequently overlooked and underemphasized.

Dr. Kirkpatrick's study also enables her to explode the myth of political women as rebels or aggressive exceptions.

> Most women in politics have led quite conventional lives. With very few exceptions they have fulfilled the traditional role of wife, mother, and good citizen in their communities. . . .

She then describes how, as their children grow older and time pressures decrease, these women decide they can do more about their various volunteer interests by running for public office.

Additional reassuring details that may help you realize you have the qualifications to succeed in politics come from the first national who's who of women in public office, conducted in 1974 and 1975 by the Center for the American Woman and Politics (C.A.W.P.), at the Eagleton Institute, Rutgers University. Moving beyond local politics into state and even national affairs, the researchers discovered that 52 percent of female state senators and a stunning 84 percent of female state representatives had *never* before held an elective office. In other words, they had moved straight from community volunteer work into successful races for state political office. At the local level, obviously, your chances for success are even higher.

Do not worry about your age or your educational background either. Among all women serving their *first* term in an elective office, 75 percent were over 40 years old. Among women mayors and state senators, a majority were over 50. As for education, though women office holders frequently do have a good education, at county and local levels most are not college graduates. Children? Again, they are apparently not a problem. Women elected officials not only have children, but also are often mothers of large families. Almost half of women state legislators have three or more children. And they are just as likely to be married and living with their husbands as are the general population of American women.

You Do Not Need a Long-Time Interest in Politics

Joan recalled her own lack of political knowledge as the two of us sat on the couch of her living room, pleasantly furnished in practical, modern furniture. "I personally had never had any interest in politics. I was a physical education teacher, and I avoided all political science courses in college because they sounded so boring."

When she moved to her present home town, a neighbor

persuaded her to join the League of Women Voters. She discovered she liked it "because there was a chance to think and use your brains." Within two years Joan was president, then president again for a second term. Each term is two years. "Six years after joining the League there I was at a kind of 'What next?' point. I'd been president twice. There wasn't any other volunteer work that interested me. So I decided to become active in politics. And just like that, I went down to a town Democratic Club meeting."

Most men and women think of the Republican and Democratic organizations of their town as closed societies. It is true that if you know someone in the group, you can request an invitation to a meeting. But it is not necessary. Anybody can attend uninvited, as Joan did. Once there, naturally, Joan knew a number of the people. That is the point! Anyone who has been active in her town in any organization eventually becomes acquainted with many people, at least by sight.

Do You Want a Career in Politics, or a Life as an Envelope-Stuffer?

"Now right here," Joan warns, "you have to make up your mind what you want to be and what you want to do." The standard political advice insists that you start as a good worker. You stuff envelopes, you make phone calls, you make coffee. *"But you have to realize that whatever level you bring yourself in on, that's the level you're going to be pegged at,"* says Joan. "If you come in as an envelope stuffer, coffee maker, and phone call maker, you're going to be stuffing envelopes, making phone calls, and brewing coffee for the rest of your political career. No one will ever see you as a possibility for a government job or as someone to help make important decisions.

"However, if you walk in with the thought in mind, 'I'm a potential candidate. I've been a leader in X town group. Consequently, I have X number of votes I can probably bring with me,' you begin at a totally different level and you take off from there. That's true of a man or a woman."

As a former League president, Joan arrived with this attitude and ready-made status. Furthermore, with an organization background she could find people who would be willing to join the Democratic Club—dues are only $3 a year—and these people would be interested in filling vacancies on the County Democratic Committee. *This is how you develop.* Joan ticked off the sequence. "First you join with your 'constituency.' Then you bring members to the political club and suggest your friends' names for vacancies as they develop.

"I would sit at meetings, listen, and participate. I didn't really understand how I was avoiding the envelope-stuffer trap. Here's a funny story that illustrates how I accidentally did it. One night during a meeting, two men who had become friends said to me, 'You know you're a terrible woman.'

" 'Why?' I asked.

" 'Don't you know you belong over there in the back with the other women talking and making coffee. Why do you always come and sit in the front row and participate just as though you belonged?' They were kidding me. It was said with good spirit. They'd noticed, but I hadn't.

"The women in the corners weren't interested in political careers. Most were wives of politicians, and that was the role they wanted. It wasn't forced on them. It was self-segregation. By thinking of themselves in those terms, they'd gravitated to the corner and powerlessness. Because I came with the idea of participating, I did so and was accepted."

At the same time, a woman who wants to become active in politics must be alert to unconscious sexism from men. At first, the men automatically cast Joan as secretary rather than decision maker. But she turned aside all requests that she take minutes with a diplomatic, "Oh, I don't know how to take minutes." When they asked her for coffee, she replied, "I make terrible coffee." It didn't take long before they stopped automatically assigning her the woman's-role tasks.

Barbara Mikulski, a Baltimore city councilwoman, echoes Joan's advice with a slight twist. She suggests that women who want to get into politics do so and not wait passively to be asked. She advises avoiding the envelope-stuffing trap by never accepting an unimportant job. If you have already been relegated to addressing envelopes, then break out "by taking over the mail room."

First Opportunity

After a few months, Joan's district county committeeman relinquished the job. Because Joan had been attending and participating in meetings, the county committee position was offered to her. It is a district committeeperson's responsibility among other duties, to become acquainted with the people in the district; to discover what their local interests are, who votes in primaries, what their party registration is; and to get out voters on election day. "I thought that would be great. I said, 'Sure.' "

Joan happened to receive the county committeewoman appointment as her first chance. But she emphasizes, "Any woman who does as I did, who joins her party, exhibits interest and works for the party, will get a job as a committeeperson or club officer or appointment of some kind. In fact, nowadays, political parties have begun actively looking for women as potential candidates.

"When I started in 1970, people were suspicious of women in politics. Men thought they couldn't attract votes, and women were hostile to the whole idea. Now there've been enough elections where women have done well or run ahead of their tickets, so that men as well as women are convinced a woman can make a strong candidate."

The national Women's Political Caucus reported that in 1974 the overall success rate for women candidates at state level and above was 60 percent. (They have neither later nor local figures.) In their book, *Clout, Womanpower, and Politics* (New York: Coward, McCann & Geoghegan, 1973) political scientist Susan Tolchin and her husband, the well-known writer Martin Tolchin, conclude after more than 200 pages of documentation and discussion that "women candidates are now finding their sex an advantage in politics and its drawbacks substantially reduced in comparison with the past." Watergate and other scandals, they report, have made people eager for alternative types of candidates, and women politicians' creuibility is high. A Louis Harris poll reveals that both men and women are coming to believe that "the country would be better off if women had more to say about politics."

Joan Masel sees the new attitude affecting her own life. "Now I get the opposite reaction from what I was getting in 1970–1972. The men and women who formerly questioned my interest in politics are now likely to tell me, 'Atta girl, Joan, go to it.'"

2
How to Get
Yourself Nominated
for a Government Office

Through Election And Appointment

Joan Masel sums it up well. "Even the woman who doesn't want to undergo the bedlam of running for an elected office can gain a position of importance in government. By establishing herself with her party, she can win office through appointment to an important town or county board or commission. *Being in politics is appointment as well as election to office! People, especially women, tend to forget that.*

"Sometimes there is tremendous competition for a certain nomination. Other times you can get it simply by being there, by having worked for your party and by offering to take the nomination. Surprisingly, there are a good number of times when it's hard to find a candidate for an elected or appointed job. Men are busy with their business careers. Women aren't aware of the opportunities. There just aren't that many interested, intelligent people working in politics. If it's your party that's in power, then your chances are good for a nomination. There's a constant supply of openings which develop on town or county boards and commissions. When your party comes to power, naturally they'll be anxious to fill those positions with people loyal to the party. Where are they going to find these loyal people? Obviously, the local Democratic or Republican clubs are the prime source of proven party devotees."

That was how Joan progressed. After six months at the political club and proving herself by working hard for the party's congressional candidate, she was offered an appointment to a

town board in addition to her party district job. She had held a
cottage party for the congressional candidate at her home, taken
him around her district, even to the town pool, and introduced
him to people, made phone calls, written letters, brought out her
district's vote. Now, *even though he lost,* the town appointment
for Joan was suggested as recognition of her efforts. It was to the
animal welfare board.

"Here again," cautions Joan, "you have to have a certain image
of what you want to do and the level you're willing to start at. I
told them I wouldn't take the animal board. If they wanted to
recognize my work, then give me a job I'm interested in and can
enthusiastically contribute to. So they came up with a position on
the town assistance (welfare) board. This board serves people.
This I took. I could have stayed there and moved up through
working for the party and seeking other appointments. However,
I happened to be interested in an elected office.

"There's such a thing as timing in politics. A woman can
sometimes take a big leap forward by being willing to run in a
hopeless race. That's how I got my election start. Six months after
I began going to meetings, nominations for town council came up.
The party was split. There was an independent who thought he
might run; the incumbent couldn't decide whether to run or not.

"During the meeting someone asked, 'Well, who's willing to
run for us?' Just as a joke, because I'd only been there six months,
I said, 'I'll run.' At the time I just wanted to give them the idea
that I might someday be a candidate.

"Then, as things turned out, the independent broke away and
ran as an independent. The incumbent decided not to run. There
I was, the only volunteer. Later, I discovered that all the
experienced politicians knew this party-split situation meant my
chances were hopeless. But I didn't know it. I ran, and, of course,
I lost."

Gateway to Nominations

"Even losing in that hopeless situation was useful. It gave me
prominence. After the election, the mayor wanted my assistance
board seat for a supporter of his who had a special interest in this

kind of work. He offered me a position on the most powerful board in town, the planning board, if I'd resign my welfare board job. Since the planning board's work was what really interested me most, I obliged.

"*Any woman who gets herself appointed to a major board or commission in her town would be in a valuable position.* You're now involved in active governing. *These are the training grounds for people who hope to run for office.* They're the next logical step after you become active politically. You speak up at meetings, you get your views in the newspapers. People in town get to know your name and know what your ideas and philosophy are. You have a chance in these boards to prove that you can accomplish something and succeed in government responsibility.

"The planning board, with its work in town planning and zoning, is a strong, visible spot that's well reported by the newspapers. A town recreation commission seat is also good. There you can become involved with children and all the parents, and you greatly broaden your contacts throughout the community. The board of adjustment, which votes on variance requests for buildings contrary to zoning regulations, is also good. Their meetings often draw crowds.

The following year, when nomination time for council candidates arrived, Joan's party appeared to have an excellent chance of winning, whereupon the party began searching for a man to run. This was back in 1972, when sentiment for women in politics was still lukewarm. Joan was stunned. "This is where the so-called behind-the-scenes struggle comes in," she says. "But a lot of it is easy to understand and arrange for yourself if you just think about it. The town Democratic Club voted for the man. But the County Committee, which in our area has the real power and where I'd nominated a lot of my friends when vacancies opened up, voted for me. So I received the nomination. This time I won.

"I wasn't really any different this year from the time I'd lost. In the interval, though, many more people became acquainted with me. They read about my work on the planning board in the town newspaper. They learned my views. They just got to recognize my name. It's exposure and getting known that's important in politics."

Other Ways to Get Nominated

1. Various towns and various parts of the country have different nominating technicalities. In a town where the local political club makes the nomination, a woman can succeed by joining the club and encouraging her friends and their husbands to join. The dues are usually a nominal two to five dollars a year. Her friends do not have to attend meetings, except for the crucial night when she needs votes for a nomination. Then they can turn out to vote for her.

2. For a woman who has some volunteer constituency but who would like to broaden her image and acquaintances, work on a town project is enormously valuable; a community recreation project such as a town pool or any civic undertaking that is important and popular is useful.

3. Another proven way is to attend town meetings and speak up. Many women (and men, too) have begun successful political careers in their towns in this fashion. There is a problem that disturbs some townspeople. The woman's comments attract others who feel as she does, and she becomes the spokesperson for the group. On the basis of that constituency, she wins a nomination and election victory. One Missouri woman I interviewed by mail sent me newspaper clippings recording her progress: she first appeared at a town council meeting as an individual citizen speaking against garden apartment zoning changes, later was spokesperson on the subject for a group of citizens, and ultimately became a successful candidate for a council seat. I also received letters and clippings from other women throughout the United States who, though they represented different issues, had followed this route to political office. Sometimes it was a school board issue, sometimes taxes, sometimes the environment, but the results were the same: a political career for the spokeswoman.

4. Simply speaking up brings results. In part, Joan won her initial appointment to the assistance board by rising at a council meeting and pointing out to the mayor that there were no women on any of the major town-governing commissions or boards.

"You can take it as a basic rule," says Joan, "that people get local nominations from political parties by attending party meetings, working for the party, having friends as members who will vote for their nomination. And you win votes in lots of other ways, from people whose cause you've stood behind when they needed a vote, from people you've helped. Most important, if you have a real political philosophy and ideas, you develop loyalty and a following simply because you do have views and you do stand for something."

Do You Have to Have Money to Be in Politics?

Some people wonder if you have to have money to be in politics. "In local politics, no. Definitely not," declares Joan. "The money politicians are said to need is used to make themselves known. There are enough avenues, such as we've discussed, available on a local level to gain exposure so that personal money isn't a necessity.

"On county or state levels it's hard to say. Sometimes a candidate's ability to help fund the campaign might be important. Sometimes not. Sometimes the candidate has qualities or stands for something attractive to voters, and the feeling is that this kind of candidate would draw money to the campaign.

"In years when your party seems to have a good chance of winning, then the county nomination can be very hard fought. Real battles for power. Then the potential ability to raise money for the campaign would be a consideration in who gets the nomination. Yet the other situation exists. As I mentioned at the beginning, sometimes a party has difficulty just finding people to run. Then money probably wouldn't be a consideration. And, of course, every election has upsets where the underdog comes through. A woman can offer herself as a candidate in these underdog races. Even if she loses, she's then established party credits for herself, as I did with my first losing race. Then she'll be in a better position the next time a potentially winning nomination is available."

Campaign Help

After you have the nomination, how do you win? Your local colleagues will have ideas for local strategy. Privately you can strengthen yourself with a series of campaign aids published especially for women who are making the transition from interested citizen to active political candidate.

Both major political parties have you in mind. The National Federation of Republican Women, 310 First Street S.E., Washington, D.C. 20003, has a very helpful basic book of ideas, *Consider Yourself for Public Office,* for one dollar. By the time *From Kitchen to Career* is in print, the *National Federation of Republican Women Campaign Manual* may also be in print and ready for shipment to you. Inquire. The Office of Women's Activities, Democratic National Committee, 1625 Massachusetts Avenue N.W., Washington D.C. 20036 has an entire kit, "Tips on Running for Public Office," which is sent upon request; it includes a model press release, "Tips for a Winning Campaign," "How to Build Precinct Strength," 'Coffee Hours for Candidates," even "Tips for a Candidate's Husband," and lots more.

The National Women's Education Fund, 1532 16th Street N.W., Washington, D.C. 20036, sounds as if it deals with schools but is really a political education organization. It is preparing an excellent campaign technique workbook, which also ought to be available by the time this book reaches you.

For ongoing information about you as a woman in politics, contact the Women's National Political Caucus, 1921 Pennsylvania Avenue, Washington N.W. 20006. Its two publications, *NWPC Newsletter* and *Women's Political Times,* give you what you need to know.

For research information about women and politics, you can turn to the Center for the American Woman and Politics (C.A.W.P.), Eagleton Institute, Wood Lawn, Neilson Campus, New Brunswick, New Jersey 08901, Dr. Ruth B. Mandel, director. (They also offer grants for research concerning women and politics.) In an interview with me, Dr. Mandel summed up the current political climate. "Every woman office holder that I have discussed this with has reported that overwhelmingly the voters are very receptive to women as candidates."

3
The Personal Side
of Being in Politics

Joan Masel paused, sat back on the brown print couch in the living room of her small ranch house, and considered the question for a long minute when I asked her, "How does being in politics affect a woman's personal life?"

"Well, some things are relatively simple and great. When I was in school, I was terrified of public speaking. Hated it. Now, of course, when any organization needs a speaker, they say, 'Get Joan.'"

"But how did you overcome your fears when you had to make your first political speech?" I asked.

"Again, the background in women's volunteer work was useful. You have to talk to be active in a woman's group. I talked as an officer of the League of Women Voters, and gradually, I guess, I just grew up and got used to it. By the time I joined the Democratic party, I was ready to go. Public speaking is just like anything else. The more you do it, the easier it becomes!

"Another thing that was simple and even kind of fun. When I was first elected councilwoman and started going to the meetings, the men were self-conscious. They did all the gallant things like holding my chair and telling me at the beginning of the meeting that my dress was pretty. There was a certain amount of kidding and wisecracking about me as a woman. Since I felt I'd never be accepted as an equal legislator as long as they went on in this way, I put a stop to it. Every time one of them told me my dress was pretty or that I looked well, I'd say, "Oh yes, and I love your tie, and how did you get that wonderful tan?' If they held my chair, then I'd hold theirs. In a little while they caught on, and everyone settled down to take care of business and relaxed. As for being squeamish about the roughness of smoke-filled rooms, etc., that idea is left over from the time when women were sheathed in a helpless-innocent stereotype. Nothing happens that would upset a modern woman."

Other female politicians find that prejudice, conscious and unconscious, requires that they look beyond an antiwoman remark to its inherent foolishness and expose it as such. As the number of women elected to office in Joan's area has increased, councilwomen from ten neighboring towns have joined for informal luncheons to trade ideas. Anita Siegenthaler remembers that in 1973, when sentiment was still ambivalent about women, she ran for a council seat and suggested to a recreation committee member that she might like to join that committee.

"We had a woman as commissioner a year ago," he retorted. "She was such a problem, we'll never have another one."

Said Anita, "If a man had not worked out, he wouldn't have said, 'We'll never appoint another man.' " That kind of prejudice has to be exposed instantly for the kind of blind foolishness it is. Surprisingly, many people—Archie Bunkers included—will see the point if someone will only show it to them.

Children and Husbands

A conference of 500 women in the Washington, D.C.-Maryland-Virginia area, sponsored by the Washington Institute for Women in Politics, were told that political decisions are made at night when the phones stop ringing. Consequently, political effectiveness for women depends on their being willing to work long hours so as to be there when power is being talked. Ann Lewis, deputy campaign manager for Senator Birch Bayh, declared that "to the extent that people get used to seeing you at night, the more they accept you."

Fortunately, the demands of local politics are considerably fewer than those of national politics. Yet when I asked Joan Masel what kind of husband and what kind of children a woman in politics needed, she laughed. "A man has to be very patient, and the children have to be independent. They can't be the kind who rely on Mommy for every little thing. Of course, if a woman's children are older, there's no problem. I started as a councilwoman when my children were eight and fourteen. I think that might have been a little early. We managed. But I think it might be better to wait till they're a little older. I'm out four, sometimes five, nights a week at meetings. It's true I don't go till eight at night, which means I see my children from three to eight every day for five hours. That's one important thing people still don't understand about women in politics." She sighed, a sigh of deep frustration. "People don't seem to realize I'm home with my children till eight o'clock at night even when I do go to meetings. But a man in politics comes home from a day at work, grabs his dinner, and leaves. He *never* sees his children. Yet it's only about the mother that people comment, 'How can she afford the time?' No one ever questions about the father."

As for husbands, Joan points out it depends on the man's own career pattern and his weekly schedule. For a woman married to a man who travels frequently for business, politics can be an ideal way to keep herself occupied and in contact with people. (Single, widowed, divorced, or separated women might feel that the regular schedule of evening political activities is an attraction.) If a man is out two, three, four nights a week for business or activities of his own, then a wife's political commitments may not be a problem. For a woman whose husband works at night, again, politics can be a happy solution with few accompanying marital inconveniences. And many men find a wife's political success intriguing because of the new social contacts and life experiences he gains. But at other times a woman politician may find her success hard on a husband. Joan sums it up, "Though most husbands of politicians that I know are truly proud of their wives' accomplishments, yet society sometimes makes it hard for these men.

"A wife can and does accompany a politician husband to endless political events. She's the second banana of her husband-wife political team. Nobody thinks about it. But men are used to being the center of attention, the leader, and the outstanding person in a situation. It's very hard on many husbands to go to a political social function where people there know his wife. They are there because his wife is who she is, and he is just-the-husband. It's only because society is not used to this kind of situation that the husband is made to feel people are questioning him because he's not the politician or the elected official. Of course, he doesn't have to go. But many husbands are torn. They're uncomfortable at the affairs. Yet neither do they want their wives going alone. Maybe this is one of those problems that will solve itself as women with careers of all kinds become common."

As women with political careers do become more common, a new breed of husband does indeed seem to be slowly evolving. In the summary reprint of the C.A.W.P. who's who of American women politicians, *Profile of Women Holding Public Office,* the authors discovered from their data that " . . . husbands, though they may require a certain amount of care and attention, on balance contribute support and services that operate to free their wives for greater political commitments." Linda Winikow, a New York state senator, provides a specific example of how this new kind of political husband is starting to function. When the legislature is in session, she leaves home on Monday morning for Albany after she sees her two young sons off to grade school. Late Wednesday night she returns. Thursday through Sunday she combines home and official duties. "My husband takes over when I am away. This was a family decision, and I couldn't do what I am doing without that kind of help." Incidentally, Linda Winikow rose to her state legislature seat by the straightforward route Joan Masel had described: She (1) joined a local campaign committee, (2) became party committeewoman, (3) led a citizens' council fight on a controversial local issue, (4) accepted an appointment to the town zoning board of appeals, (5) ran for and won a town council seat, (6) ran for and won a county legislature seat, (7) ran for and won a state legislature seat. Moreover, the *time elapsed from the local town zoning board appointment to the legislature of the Empire State was just five years.*

Personal and Emotional Point of View

Says Joan, "From a personal, emotional point of view, you have to develop a thick skin. You have to expect criticism and learn not to take it to heart. Though I guess it's not different from a woman who is or wants to be an executive in business. Also you'd meet this kind of pressure, criticism, and gossip about you in any organization that you belong to. Probably many women are already veterans of in-fighting politicking from their years as officers of their organizations, or this even happens in churches and synagogues when a new minister or rabbi is hired or some group tries to dislodge the current cleric or change church or synagogue policy on some issue.

"So, probably many women who might think of entering politics have already survived some pretty tough bouts, and it won't be that new to them.

"One thing that again may be similar to business office politicking is the fact that, just as in business, in politics you can't hold a grudge. This is different from the usual woman's idea of loyalty to her friends and antipathy to those who have opposed her ideals or her causes. Even though you have these terrific battles with people, you can't think of it in terms of 'I'll get even with them.' The person who is your enemy this year may be your very good friend for a new situation or cause next year. This idea of quickly forgetting current disagreements may be new to a woman. At times it seems two-faced, but that's the way politics from local to national functions. Each new issue brings new alignments, and you have to be prepared to accept your last week's enemy as your new ally.

"On a personal level you have to enjoy people immensely, enjoy meeting, talking, and dealing with them. An introvert is not going to be happy as a politician. But an extrovert can love it. To me, what I enjoyed most about campaigning was knocking on people's doors and just talking to them.

"The first couple of times you do it, it's not easy even for a person like me who has the temperament for it. But you find that, contrary to what you might expect, most people are happy to see you. They're very flattered at the idea of a candidate coming to speak to them personally. There are so few people who've ever had a prospective mayor or congressperson or even a councilperson come to their house that they're usually thrilled. To me, and to many other women in politics, this constantly being with people, combined with having a genuine power share in high-level, major decisions, becomes a fascinating job and way of life with endless possibilities for advancement."

SECTION VI

HIGH-PAYING JOBS AND CAREERS BY AVOIDING THE STANDARD "WOMEN'S JOBS"

1
Where the Jobs
and Money Are

A few years ago a riddle spread across the United States, bewildering almost everyone who attempted it. Probably you yourself were bedeviled by it. If you solved it at the first try, you were the rare exception. It went like this: A man and his son are out driving in their automobile when their car is struck by a truck. The father is killed, and the son is rushed to a hospital emergency room. As the surgeon is about to operate, a nurse exposes the injured boy's face; the surgeon halts and says, "I cannot operate on this boy. He is my son." Question: How could this be?

From one end of the United States to the other, people who were educated, ingenious and skilled in puzzles wrestled with the question and failed.

Whether we realize it or not, all of us are to some extent limited by inculcated sex-role expectations—even those who consider themselves open-minded and liberated. A letter to the editor in a national magazine by a woman who described herself as a long-time advocate of sexual equality recounted her chagrin during a hospital stay. When a male nurse appeared with the bedpan she had requested, the lady who had believed herself totally free of sexually stereotyped ideas was so startled that, "as in an animated cartoon, every drop of urine fled my bladder and raced back to the kidneys."

A friend who is active in local women's rights affairs remembers that the first time she saw a uniformed woman mail carrier she was frozen in place with shock, then instantly felt ridiculous. Certainly she believes women should be mail carriers if they wish.

"But I'd never seen one. And I guess I automatically was surprised."

My own proof of how very blinded we can be by our sex-role conditioning occurred last summer in a shopping-center parking lot. A girl of about 13 was walking toward us wearing a shiny jersey top with a number on it and what looked like knee-length pants. Accustomed to the speed with which teen-age clothing fads appear and disappear, I realized that though I had lived through the hippie look, jungle look, Nehru look, and a dozen others, this was a brand-new costume. Turning to my thirteen-year-old son, I pointed out the girl. "What do you call an outfit like that?"

He glanced at her. "A Little League uniform." he said.

I, who the year before had written a piece for our local newspaper defending girls' right to play Little League baseball, was unable to recognize the result when I looked at it. A lifetime of social conditioning had prepared me to disbelieve my own convictions when I saw them in action.

That most of us do have a compartmentalized, narrow view of what are appropriate female and male activities is massively proved by Bureau of the Census findings: Though there are 250 distinct occupations listed in its tabulations, half of all women workers were employed in only 21 of them, with a heavy emphasis on clerical jobs. Male workers were much more widely dispersed, with 50 percent of the men in 65 occupations. Bureau of Labor Statistics economists explain, "The high concentration of women workers is due to many factors. Some were valid at one time; few are valid today." They point out that the limited kinds of jobs in which women are employed are often extensions of the work women have done in the home. But, more important, widely held prejudices that some jobs are feminine while others are masculine have artificially restricted women's jobs far beyond limits set by job requirements or working conditions."

The practical career and income results of this stereotyped thinking is summed up in a one-paragraph squib published by the respected business magazine, *Personnel Journal.* Under a sardonic headline, "You've Come a Long Way, Baby?" (note the question mark added to that familiar ad slogan), they report that the latest Statistical Abstract of the United States Census Bureau "put the male's median salary at 108% over his female counterpart's and that this is the same ratio that existed back in 1960."

Employment discrimination provides only a limited explanation of why women's income has failed to rise in proportion to men's. As long as women congregate in their traditional occupations—as clerical workers, salesclerks, and helpers of various kinds—they will inevitably draw the modest salaries these occupations command. *Only by avoiding stereotyped thinking and by entering the jobs where the money is can you obtain what your life experience and abilities entitle you to.*

In addition to substantial monetary loss, unemployment can be another result of stereotyped thinking. Though women's current passion for jobs and careers represents new modes of feminine thinking, most of the newly motivated have stampeded into the *traditional* "female" occupations and professions. College women have overwhelmingly chosen to become teachers, social workers, library workers, home economists, and medical laboratory technicians. The jam in teaching is already well publicized. Last September, in a situation typical of the entire United States, the superintendent of schools in our town received 1,200 applications for the 20 teaching positions he had open. Experts categorize it as the worst teaching job market since the Great Depression. Given our current demographics, the discouraging job outlook for teachers will continue. Department of Labor forecasts warn that at present rates all "women's professions," with the exception of secretary, will soon be overpopulated. As the labor experts sum it up for you: "Many more women must prepare to enter work outside the traditional women's occupations *if they are to find jobs in keeping with their ability* [emphasis added]."

Over these years of living and homemaking, you have, without realizing it, been preparing yourself to enter many well-paying jobs other than the stereotyped "female" ones. Now we are going to discover which of these positions best suit you.

First, in case you are still wondering about that riddle, the answer that eluded so many millions of intelligent adults would be obvious to any three-year-old who had not yet been brainwashed into sex-role thinking. If the boy's father was killed in the car, the surgeon must, of necessity, be the other parent, his mother.

2
But What Occupations
Are Women Really Suited For?

Though she was desperate to find something to occupy her time, Amy Spielen nevertheless shied away from clerical work. "It was the only thing I seemed prepared for. Yet the idea of sitting at a desk all day depressed me." While she stalled, she busied herself hanging wallpaper for a friend who had moved to a new home. Years before, when she had first married, Amy had taught herself wallpapering. "My husband doesn't want to have anything to do with such things." She had been doing it ever since for herself, her mother, sister, mother-in-law. Other women in the Michigan housing development admired the rooms Amy had completed for her friend and began calling Amy to ask about rates. "Rates? What did I know?" says Amy. "It had never occurred to me. It was just something I did as part of my housewife life." Three years later she runs a very profitable business with a housewife partner, who is another wallpaper enthusiast. "I learned you can charge by the roll or by the hour. I charge by the roll." Amy also discovered that the average housewife much prefers a competent woman worker. The housewife knows she need not hover over a craftswoman in order to guard her furniture and drapes from careless mishandling. "And housewives often feel more comfortable alone all day in their homes with another woman than with a strange man." Word of mouth from satisfied customers, supplemented by a small regular ad in the town weekly, bring Amy and her partner more business than they can handle.

Since the early 1970s it has been almost impossible to read your local newspaper without coming upon sporadic "gee-whiz" news features about women like Amy Spielen, who are developing successful careers in a "man's job." In addition to the standard occupations like engineer, architect, lawyer, we read about plumbers, firewomen, policewomen, female telephone installers, traveling saleswomen, pastors, assembly-line forewomen, bus drivers, real estate tycoons, and so on. Diverse as these articles are, through each runs a common theme: The woman who is the subject of the article is "different." She is an "unusual" woman. Yes, the articles suggest that some other women may be following her into this "male" career, but they are all "unusual" women.

This is superb confirmation of a major criticism of the American press. So occupied are they with the immediate hot story of that day that they rarely make clear the story's fundamental meaning.

The correct meaning of these thousands of individual gee-whiz-look-what-job-that-lady-has stories is that, like men, women have a spectrum of abilities and interests. This statement has often been made. It is the translation into action that is holding us up.

The point is: it is not the rare woman who has these abilities. It is the *usual* woman. *This is simply the first time in history that women have had the social sanction to use these natural abilities of theirs.*

The chances are high that you have a cluster of natural aptitudes, which, together with your life experiences, fit you for a well-paying, so-called "masculine," job.

The Johnson O'Connor Research Foundation, a nonprofit, nationwide research organization which has tested more than a half million men and women for work aptitudes during the last half century, has discovered that *more* women than men have the natural abilities needed to succeed as bankers, managers, executives, politicians, chemists, physicians, lawyers, insurance adjusters, police officers, and workers in a variety of trades and crafts. Despite what this study shows to be their natural talents, however, women have not entered these occupations in meaningful numbers because they have been conditioned to believe that women lack the necessary abilities and that these are therefore "male" jobs.

Once upon a time, people universally believed the world was

flat. It didn't make the world flat. It just made all the believers wrong. Similarly, the belief that women *in general* don't have certain aptitudes hasn't stripped women of these faculties. It just makes everyone who holds that belief wrong.

So cockeyed are the effects of sex-role conditioning that we constantly hear and read of able women denying their own innate powers. Next to me is a newspaper clipping in which a successful young woman in her 20s, a nuclear and biomedical engineer who is part of a team designing a nuclear power plant, is quoted as saying she likes her work because working in a male environment makes her think more logically.

Damnation!!

Vast research statistics prove that the young lady thinks in a logical fashion because she, like a very high percentage of women, has a natural aptitude for thinking logically, while a good percentage of men just as naturally have no capacity whatsoever for it. How does she believe she managed to become a competent nuclear engineer? Through osmosis, by sitting in a roomful of male students, or by having the necessary ingredients inside her head? Logic, like every capability, is related not to sex but to individual talent.

Women's Job Aptitudes Compared to Men's Job Aptitudes

The Johnson O'Connor findings are impressive. Working with the 21 vocational aptitudes for which they have been able to devise valid tests, the researchers have ascertained that the percentage of women possessing certain talents not only equals but, for some talents, exceeds the percentage of men who possess these abilities.

Since the Foundation has been testing for more than fifty years (does it carry more weight if we say more than half a century?), it has been able to check its deductions against the subjects' lives. In follow-up surveys of subjects' careers, the accuracy of the Foundation's vocational analyses has been confirmed. Overall, for the 21 aptitudes, the researchers report that 13 revealed "no discernible sex difference." As high a proportion of women as of men have the following abilities:

Analytical (logical) reasoning
Eyedness
Foresight
Inductive reasoning
Memory for design
Number memory
Objective personality
Subjective personality
Pitch discrimination
Rhythm memory
Timbre discrimination
Tonal memory
Tweezer (digital) dexterity

In his excellent article on the Foundation's discoveries, "The Potential of Women," author Jon Durkin notes that, of the remaining 8 aptitudes, women excel at 6, and men, at only 2. By excel, the Foundation means that a higher proportion of one sex than of the other has the ability. For example, structural visualization is one of the two at which men excel. One man in two has the ability, whereas only one woman in four possesses it. But the 25 percent of women with structural visualization *are as talented in it* as are the 50 percent of men with the ability. Male or female, those who have it, have it! It is only that fewer women than men demonstrate that they can think in three dimensions, a talent which is required for success in such areas as the physical sciences, engineering, architecture, city planning, building, and mechanics.

Grip is the second aptitude at which men excell—Surprise! Surprise! Grip is useful for construction work and other strength-related duties. Even here, though, there are certainly some women strong enough to succeed at various physical tasks if such tasks interest them. (Indeed there are; an Associated Press story told of the 1,000 women who worked alongside 15,000 men laying the Alaska pipeline. "They're some of our best workers," said the project boss. He added that they made the same pay as the men; for example, $1,000 per 70-hour week as truck drivers.)

That leaves us six aptitudes at which women excel; that is, more women than men have high ability for the following skills:

1. Abstract Visualization: This skill is important in banking, management, politics, writing, and various nontechnical professions. Whereas 75 percent of women possessed it, only 50 percent of men did. Mr. Durkin writes, "Theoretically at least, there ought to be more women in management than men."

2. Ideaphoria: a measure of the rate of flow of ideas used in activities involving persuasion and verbal fluency. It is helpful in sales, teaching, writing, and advertising.

3. Silograms: the ability to form associations easily between known and unknown words. This talent is necessary for acquiring professional terminology in chemistry, medicine, law, and languages.

4. Observation: the ability to perceive small changes, alterations in physical details. It is useful for insurance adjustment, police work, and, of course, factory inspection.

5. Finger Dexterity: This skill is commonly utilized by women for all kinds of low-paid work, such as factory assembly, but is just as applicable to occupations like dentistry, surgery, business machine repairs, T.V. repairs, and auto mechanics.

6. Graphoria: clerical speed and efficiency. We all know how women normally use this ability. But, says the Foundation, the same skills are involved in high-paying accounting, auditing, statistics, and actuarial work. We have already learned that as many girls as boys have natural "number memory."

The Department of Labor, using its own statistics and tests, reports that three women in five have the talents to succeed at engineering and science. In addition, the aptitudes required for success in trades and crafts such as repair of office machines, household appliances, radios, T.V.s, autos, and aircraft are found as frequently among girls as among boys (that finger dexterity again). Since these trades require only light strength, are usually carried out indoors, are very well paid, and promise an insatiable capacity to absorb practitioners, the Department recommends them to women. Moreover, these occupations are portable. Wherever a woman and her family may move, she is immediately in demand.

Dentistry and medicine make clear that it is society's expectation—not natural capacity—that usually determines a girl's career choice. The American Dental Association has commented that dentistry is particularly convenient for a married woman because she can have her office in her home, make her own office hours, take advantage of women's smaller hand and employ the finger dexterity so many women possess. The Dental Association then wonders aloud why female dentists represent barely 1 percent of American dentists, whereas in some countries 80 percent of dentists are women. In medicine the same situation exists. The United States ranks with Madagascar, Viet Nam and Spain as having the lowest proportion of women doctors, about 7 percent of American physicians. Is it really that American women are 79 percent less able than foreign women to learn dentistry? Or is this a smashing example of women's limiting their career horizons by thinking in stereotypes?

3
How to Get Started
in a Nontraditional Career

Some women may have to obtain a degree in such disciplines as law, medicine, architecture, and engineering to use their innate talents. Many others, as we have discovered, like Marian Burden, Harriet Lefkowith, Gloria Brager, Adele Lerner, and Pat Dimitri, have had sufficient preparation through living, volunteer work, and aid to their husband's careers to step immediately into executive and administrative posts.

Other women find that as soon as they begin to think nontraditionally and move their minds away from the standard "women's" jobs, they realize that some of the ordinary office jobs they have had can be used as springboards to much better opportunities. Louise Higgins had been a clerk/typist/secretary in a small insurance office for years. Her "ordinary everyday" job had magnificently prepared her when it finally occurred to her that she ought to stop processing salesmen's commission accounts for her lowly clerk's salary; she decided instead to take her lively personality and go out and earn those commissions for herself by becoming an insurance saleswoman. As long ago as 1973, a major life insurance firm, Fidelity Union Life, was putting forth promotional material, saying,

> We believe women are a tremendous source of professional talent for the insurance industry. That's why we're aggressively seeking those who have the potential. When you're evaluating professions, consider insurance potential compared with other fields.

It went on to report that, according to the *U.S. Occupational Outlook Handbook, 1972–73* (inflation would raise everything proportionally),

> Starting insurance agents earn between $8,000–$20,000. An established insurance agent earns $30,000 or more. A starting real estate person earns between $7,000–$12,000, while a high school teacher earns about $10,000 and starting stenographers employed by the federal government earn $5,212.

Mary Anne Wexler had been a third assistant in a local advertising firm. When she abandoned her stereotyped, "feminine" job ideas and began thinking nontraditionally, she took her general advertising experience ("whatever everyone else didn't want to do got dumped on me") and a group of campaign ideas she had developed for her job interview, and applied for executive director of her town's chamber of commerce. Mary Anne's "town" is really a city with a population of 40,000 and a city-sized business district to match. It is an important, well-paying, prestigious job that she won and now holds.

When she realized she was never going to be promoted to anything, Caroline Jacowski took her "ordinary" office experience as a Spanish-English typist/clerk with an import-export firm and approached a new competitor who was glad to hire her as a knowledgeable assistant. Today, she is a one-third partner in the business.

Janet Jones, a partner in the New York executive recruiting firm Management Woman, suggests that moving outside women's traditional occupations may be the quickest way to move up through the ranks. She advises going where other women have not gone. Choose things such as labor relations or sales management, where there are few women. Once in a nontraditional field, if you are competent, you are also visible and therefore eminently promotable by companies feeling public and legal pressures to promote women. Juliette Moran, executive vice-president of the giant G.A.F. Corporation, suggests, "If you're executive bound, avoid steno, typing, and other stereotyped specialties; they are a one-way ticket to the Land of the Forgotten. Let your smartness show. I know it is supposed to cause resentment in others. But people resent smart alecks, not smart producers. Good entry points for the female executive today are mathematics and computer technology." Gertrude McWilliams, senior vice-president of Campbell, Ewald Company, Detroit, Michigan, suggests you will best help yourself move into responsible positions that are not traditionally "feminine" by searching for strong, competent people as your bosses. They will allow you to become better without their feeling threatened."

Just as some women will require formal college training to enter a profession, so, too, some women may have to attend trade schools or join formal apprentice programs to develop a career in a trade. But in the trades, as in executive work, you may be able to bypass the formal study by drawing on your past everyday experiences.

Many, like Amy Spielen with her wallpapering talent, are already well prepared by their years of "just living." Pat Mandel, a New Jersey housewife in her 30s, loves cars and motors. "They turn me on. If you want to make me happy, show me a foreign car with an oil leak." Mrs. Mandel learned by watching at her husband's automotive repair shop. Others learn from books, from brothers, fathers, or by simple curiosity. Arden Scott, a young mother of four, watched the plumbers who worked at the family farmhouse. She now operates a thriving home plumbing repair business, often bringing the newest baby along. Sandra Gourley, a divorced young mother of three, was hired as a model by Rockwell Manufacturing Company, a power tool concern. Accidentally discovering she was using power tools at home as a hobby, they gave her a new job as consumer adviser and sent her touring at a far higher salary giving demonstrations of equipment. An acquaintance of ours does plastering and inside and outside house painting "for relaxation." Her family buys and renovates old houses and sells them at a profit. Her husband's craft contributions are minimal. "I adore doing it. He doesn't," the lady declares. Another housewife builds fine furniture. She has turned herself into a skilled carpenter. No one knows the exact number of woodworking craft hobbyists who are women, but they are not rare. If any of these women ever want outside careers, they are well prepared to do work they enjoy at high pay, unless they disappear into dead-end clerical jobs because it doesn't occur to them to use the skills acquired during the years spent at home "doing nothing."

Betty Katzman owns her own building contracting firm. It is an occupation that requires entrepreneurial, executive, and professional technical knowledge. She gained each of the necessary skills by herself in her daily life. When Betty and her husband were unable to contract for their home at a price they could afford, Betty became the contractor. By reading and talking to people, she gradually learned the business. As contractor, she had their house built and then had an addition constructed. By then, experienced and trial-and-error wise she recognized what she had to offer. Now, she contracts with plumbers, masons, and carpenters, then coordinates, supervises, expedites supplies, and solves on-the-job problems as her customers' houses are built. At 33, with three daughters, she has launched herself on an exciting, very remunerative career.

More Nonstereotyped Ideas

En route to higher pay and to a job and career compatible with their natural capacities, women are going in two directions: from office work to "male" handcrafts, repair work, and building trades, and from routine low-paying typing and clerical work to supervisory, administrative, and staff positions. With government equal opportunity pressure on them to open "male" occupations to women, companies are often very receptive to the woman who *applies* for a job that is not traditionally feminine. The important word in that sentence is "applies." We are not yet in that utopian age when the world will come to us.

Talk to your men friends and acquaintances. Ask what jobs their companies are hiring and training men for. If you consider with an open mind, you will realize that few, if any, of these positions are intrinsically masculine. Women just have not thought of applying for them before. What talents do the men who are being hired have? Perhaps you have similar ones. Do the new male employees have to be trained for their new work? If so, their lack of experience may instantly make you as qualified as they. You both have to learn. Age, too, may be irrelevant.

The Great Middle-aged Job Shuffle

In what is coming to be a commonplace American pattern of male career change at middle age (as documented by the Family Service Association of America), a fifty-year-old Florida man recently moved from discount store manager to police radio officer. Tiring of the pressure of retail hours, he took the county police radio exam and now is delighted with his new work as civilian police dispatcher and nerve center for citizens calling for police help. Besides doing interesting work, he has good pay with rich civil service fringe benefits, including town-paid family medical service, family eyeglasses, and dental service. The homemaker who at mid-life wants to enter the work force is making the same kind of complete job change as this man arranged for himself. Yet, despite the similarity of their job shifts, how many women would think to inquire into the whole range of local, state, and federal job openings. Or would such women have eyes only for those labeled "clerical"?

There are literally hundreds of thousands of civil service jobs: municipal, county, state, and federal. In some parts of the United States you will find additional separate employment jurisdictions such as school districts, state and community colleges, and health institutes. All have interesting, well-paying, varied jobs *other* than typing and filing (which are usually the lowest paid slots). You will find such positions as sign designer, processor and letterer; right-of-way negotiator (real estate); confidential aide, field representative, county board of taxation; chauffeur, investigator, narcotics task force; as well as numerous openings for teachers, social workers, bookkeepers, nurses, lawyers, dieticians, youth workers, and supervisory positions such as freeholder director or supervisor of central mailing room. (Do you automatically think of the job titles that specify "supervisor" or "director" as men's work? Why?)

You can obtain information on current municipal, county, and state examinations by phoning your local town clerk or the clerk at your county seat. They will tell you which office handles exams in your community. Visit it and collect the information you need; you'll probably be able to to verify for yourself that all these groups are under strong pressure to conform to affirmative action requirements to hire women.

At our county office, the director of personnel told me, "For years we didn't allow women the good-paying cancellation clerk (mortgage cancellation administration) jobs because mortgage books weigh forty pounds, and it was officially believed women therefore couldn't handle the work. Now one of our best cancellation clerks is a 105-pound woman who slings those books around as if they were Kleenex boxes. We were made to realize that women lug more than 40 pounds with toddlers, groceries, laundry." Traffic analyst was another job he mentioned as an example of how civil service has had its consciousness raised. The traffic analyst is the person who sits by the side of the highway counting traffic when new roads are planned (at much better pay than routine clerical workers). "We never would give that to a woman because the theory was women would be afraid of being raped. Well, of course, now there are women police officers, state troopers, and besides who's going to rape her in the middle of traffic?"

Yet, when I pressed him, the personnel director had to admit that though civil service now accepts candidates on ability alone, women themselves are still wearing mental blinders. By and large, women are not taking advantage of the wide new opportunities. Though all exams are open to all, most female applicants are still appearing, as of yore, only for the "traditionally female," low-paying, bottom-rung jobs. Why?

The director explained that civil service offers an additional attraction to the middle-aged woman. Private industry rarely allows a post-50-year-old new employee (either man or woman) to join the pension plan. However, civil service jurisdictions will often allow a new employee to enter its pension system all the way to age 60. "We just hired two women this week, age 55 and 57," the director said. "They'll be able to join the pension plan and can look forward to automatic pay increases the whole time they work, two things they might never be able to obtain at their ages in private industry."

For federal job openings in your area, look under "United States" in your telephone book. There, usually in a box labeled "Frequently Called Numbers," you will find "Federal Job Information Center" and an "800" number for your area. The "800" number means you pay no toll.

To prepare for local or federal examinations, you can find booklets, published by Arco and other companies, covering almost every kind of position. They provide you with typical exam questions and answers for that job. You can purchase them at local bookstores or ask the clerk at the office when you pick up the job information. Undoubtedly, the clerk has heard this question hundreds of times before and will know where in the neighborhood you can locate the study material you need.

How Men and Other Women Will React to Your Nonstereotype Occupation

A magazine cartoon shows one little girl saying to another, "By the time we grow up there won't be any 'firsts' left." That time is almost here. North Carolina and California have had women as chief justices of the state supreme court. New York now has a woman as lieutenant governor, and Connecticut, a woman as governor. Women are also bank presidents, coal miners, cattle buyers, sewer supervisors, ministers, rabbis, generals, admirals, sky marshals, FBI agents, truck drivers, professional sports referees, steel workers, foreign diplomats, state troopers, cable installers, jackhammer operators, private guards in airports and banks, blacksmiths, auctioneers, foresters, farm managers, concrete finishers, baggagewomen, astronauts, aviators, and navigators.

There are now probably some women in almost every occupation you can name. In short, if you follow where your talents, life experience, and inclination lead you, you may still be a pioneer of sorts, but you need not be concerned that you will be considered "odd." Instead, as a lead article in *The Wall Street Journal* reported, women working in nonstereotyped occupations are usually envied for the high pay they command.

Betsy Medgar, a photo-journalist who spent a year traveling the United States interviewing and photographing women who hold what were once considered men's jobs, reached a blanket conclusion. After talking to an oil rig "roughneck," wheat farmer, pilot, railroad engineer, blacksmith, clown, lobsterwoman, and many others, she says that though men in trades and other physical skill jobs may have set macho attitudes, it is often easier for women to be accepted in these occupations than in high-level white collar positions. "Getting into a white collar job is easier," she said, "but once you're in it, a lot more personal and political games can be played, making it not so clear what the job is. In production trades and production jobs, what's required of any given worker is very clear. When a woman proves she can produce, she usually is accepted."

If macho-minded men can realize that a woman can succeed at any job she has the interest in and aptitude for, are you still going to doubt it?

What have you always enjoyed puttering at? Helping with? Doing? Indoors or outdoors? What kinds of jobs do *men* hold using these skills and interests? Why can't you make yourself a career out of your competency, your years of developing it on your own?

The idea of men's occupations and women's occupations, like the idea of the pancake-shaped world, is a mistaken notion. There are only jobs and careers for people.

SECTION VII

EVEN NONEXISTENT OR RUSTY SKILLS CAN MEAN A MIDDLE- OR TOP-LEVEL JOB

1
To See Yourself
as Others See You

Many of us shudder delicately when we are reminded of the following lines and silently respond. "No thank you! I may not like what I find out about myself."

> Oh would some power the giftie give us
> To see ourselves as others see us!*

Yet it might be worthwhile to cease our shivering and seek that "giftie" of seeing ourselves as others see us. At women's centers, the crush of women who are searching for career direction has yielded an interesting discovery. At this transitional stage in their lives, when women need to be supremely aware and confident of their abilities, their self-esteem is likely to be at a lifetime low.

After a bruising interview or two with employment agencies, a woman is often ready to accept gratefully any bone of a job tossed at her, no matter how far below the level of her interests or abilities it may be!

How different her life would be if instead of settling for that scrap of a low-paying job, a woman had someone who would make her see herself clearly and help her appraise her real job potential. Emily Menninger stumbled into this kind of good fortune. *Her experiences have value for every woman who believes she has "no skills." The details of the job each woman ultimately*

* "To a Louse" by Robert Burns; spelling partially anglicized.
"Oh wad some power the giftie gie us
To see ourselves as others see us!"

obtains will, of course, vary. But you can take Emily's "accidental good luck" and deliberately cause it to happen to you. This chapter explains how.

As Emily put it, "I felt I could not even apply for any job. I had absolutely no tangible skills. I went back to my college placement service; I graduated twenty-five years ago with a B.A. degree. A very nice young lady interviewer trying to be helpful told me that for someone forty-six years old she thought I was 'holding up very well.' She told me to write a resume and try to act less timid and maybe something could be done for me. I never wrote the resume. I couldn't come up with any specific skills. All I had was a certain amount of intelligence, maturity, willingness to learn on the job. Willingness to learn is the main thing anyone without a skill has to rely on. But where are you going to find takers?"

To See Ourselves as Others See Us

After weeks of dallying, Emily visited her premarriage employer, a credit card firm where she had checked references for new applications. "All we need is someone part-time, no benefits, and the salary is clerical," they said. "I'll take it," she answered.

At home Emily telephoned one of her good friends, Jeanette, and discussed her new job with her. As friends do, Jeanette later mentioned it to her husband, James. "A part-time clerical job? Emily's capable of much better things," he said. "Let her come work for me. I can use her to monitor the foreign offices' reports."

"When I heard about James's offer," says Emily, "I was thrilled but frightened. Very frightened. James is vice-president of European operations of a multinational corporation which manufactures a wide range of consumer and industrial products. Its headquarters is here in the United States. He's responsible for total cash flow of all the overseas branches. I had one course in money and banking in college and hated it. But James said I'd be an administrative assistant, start with the monitoring, and let the job grow. No typing. I even have the help of a secretary for my reports."

Emily remembers, "I was so scared at the thought of such a challenging job I called my doctor and for the first time in my life asked for tranquilizers. It took me easily six to eight months till I felt I had a firm grasp of what I was supposed to be doing. The first few months I felt like a little girl, timid and so ignorant.

"It's a very big impersonal place. What I was being taught was very complex, and I was so unsure of myself it interfered with my ability to hear and absorb. The man who taught me did the best he could, but, after all, he has an M.B.A. degree (master of business administration) and management training, as well as years of experience, and here he's trying to teach parts of all this to a middle-aged lady with no background whatsoever.

"Yet all those months, though I was frightened, I was also happy and excited to be there. James thought I could do it. And I was going to do it."

She did. A year after she began, Emily received a raise. "Is it automatic or on merit?" she asked.

"When it comes to money, nothing here is automatic," she was told. "You're doing a good job."

In the three years since, Emily has mastered her initial assignment as watchdog of the reams of reports, presented in numbers not words, that come from the foreign branches. It is her task to analyze these reports and ferret out where company budgets and policies are being tinkered with in order to further the aims or image of an overseas subsidiary. And her duties have grown. She researches and keeps track of price patterns of major currencies to assist the corporation in determining its short-term monetary transactions. She has developed a complicated ongoing report of key indicators in the Common Market for those industries related to the operation of the corporation's subsidiaries in those countries. "No one ever showed me how to research this. Here my B.A. background in use of research sources was valuable."

"Had you ever done anything outstanding in community or volunteer work that made clear you had this ability?" I asked.

She brushed a strand of her short salt-and-pepper hair from her forehead. "No. I'd been part of volunteer projects, but nothing as a leader. I guess it was just a fluke that I got this job. Through our families' friendship over the years, Jeanette and James came to the conclusion I had some intelligence. When the situation arose, he felt I could do the job."

But was it a fluke? Or was it an example of those around Emily having the "giftie" of seeing her abilities more clearly than she herself could?

Opportunity Knocks Often, But Most of Us Laugh It Off the Doorstep

It is not true that opportunity knocks only once; it knocks all the time. But most of us laugh it off the doorstep. "Oh, I couldn't," we say. Or, "You're kidding." Or, "What me! Oh, never." Then we instantly forget about it.

By listening to your friends' image and view of you (as Emily did), you can sometimes discover you do have a very marketable talent. Teresa Cullen was newly widowed, with a reasonably adequate financial cushion, but she was frantic to find something to fill her time. An outgoing, gregarious woman, she had numerous women friends. She belonged to a penny poker club, a bowling league, a swimming pool–cabana club. Yet she kept telling friends, "I need a part-time job with people. But what can I do?" She had married immediately after high school graduation and had never held a job. One day as Teresa and a friend strolled through a department store, they passed a counter where a woman was demonstrating and talking about a kitchen appliance. "You'd be good at that," her friend told Teresa. "Me?" laughed Teresa. "I'd be scared to death."

"No, you wouldn't. You'd love it," said her friend.

Teresa laughed and they walked on. That evening, sitting alone before her T.V., Teresa remembered the incident. Next day she returned to the store, luckily found the demonstrator still there, and asked, "How do I apply for a job like this?" (If the demonstrator had been evasive, Teresa could have asked the department buyer.)

Teresa is a demonstrator now, and she does love it. Four afternoons a week, moving in a circuit through different stores, she talks and demonstrates. She has spent 32 years in a kitchen and is at home with any kitchen gadget or kitchen conversation.

Moreover, Teresa likes, craves, needs people; her warmth and interest in people make her an ideal demonstrator. She has a job for which her life experience has uniquely qualified her.

Teresa's friend instinctively saw her potential and suggested an opportunity for using it whereas Teresa, unable to see herself as others did, passed blindly by.

"You know they're starting a program to train teacher's aides. The pay is eight thousand dollars a year for a nine-to-two day," a neighbor told Marie Linck as they stood in line at the supermarket. "You'd be good at that."

"Me? Oh, I couldn't do that," Marie declared.

And the conversation passed to other things. This is usually how such conversations go. In a fleeting moment, a suggestion reveals the image others have of us, a suggestion that most of us ignore.

Learn to listen for these hints, and instead of crushing them, nurture them. Crush instead your urge to deprecate them. Ask, "Why do you think I'd be good at it?" The answer may give you a view of yourself that should have been obvious to you but was not.

If Marie had asked, her neighbor might have said, "Weren't you always volunteering for class mother and for class trips when your children were little? You work with the church youth groups. You always seem to enjoy it. Isn't that perfect for becoming a teacher's aide?"

"But I don't have two years of college," Marie might have answered.

"You don't need that for an aide."

"Oh, I thought you did. Maybe I'll find out about it. I would like it."

At any rate, Marie later chose to cultivate rather than ignore her friend's casual comment, and thus accomplished two things: She began to see her experience living at home as potential for a new job and eliminated erroneous ideas she had had about what a particular job requires. You can do the same.

Friends, Acquaintances, and a Job for You

Going back to Emily Menninger and her high-paying, prestigious job, can we honestly say that she "invented" her job? Yes. Emily accidentally used some of the valuable techniques you can *deliberately* use to invent a job for yourself, even if you feel you have "no skills."

First, as we discussed, Emily responded to and took seriously her friend's high appraisäl of her ability. When Jeanette first reported that James thought she could monitor foreign money reports, Emily might have retreated and insisted, "I could never learn that. I had banking in college for one term and hated it. Tell James thanks, but I couldn't do it." And that would have been the end of it.

Think back. Have you sloughed off suggestions with words like these? Even if Emily (or you) finally gave up on the job, it would represent that recent experience that so impresses employment agencies and employers.

Second, Emily told her friends, Jeanette among them, that she was job hunting. For Emily, the feedback was spectacularly quick. She told Jeanette one afternoon and three days later received a job offer. It may take you longer, but remember that friends and acquaintances have had a chance to develop a good opinion of your intelligence, competence, and reliability whereas strangers or employment agencies have not. To tell strangers that you are reliable is often meaningless. They have no way of knowing how true it is. A friend has. When a job's basic requirements are intelligence and reliability—qualities not so easy for an employer to come by—you are a proven quantity to a friend. Even though you lack a specific skill, to them you are worth training.

Understanding How to Extract Hidden Opportunities from the Job Market

In his respected industry guidebook, *The Professional Job Changing System*, Robert J. Jameson, who has held a variety of impressive executive and consultant positions explains, "Only a small fraction of available positions are ever advertised." He says,

> The job market is archaic and inefficient. ... At any given moment firms with attractive positions are unable to fill their jobs, while at the same time individuals who would like new employment are unaware such openings exist. One key point for you to remember is that even in times of high unemployment there are still thousands of available jobs for those who know how to find them.

Eli Djeddah, who has headed five of the major branches of the well-known executive search organization Bernard Haldane Associates, has placed approximately 5,000 people during his career. In his book *Moving Up*, he gives a precisely quantified account of the value of personal acquaintances in job hunting. Djeddah wrote his book for men, not housewives. Yet his facts are as applicable to you as to any man.

> The most important thing to understand is that in the unpublished area—80% of the job market—about half of the jobs available to you are potential jobs, not current jobs. They are jobs which might not even exist. But potential jobs can be created; *three out of ten are* [emphasis added]. The created job is the prime job, because you build it with the person who is going to employ you. There is no competition. No salary or other conditions are present. Everything is open to negotiation.

The created job is the "prime job," Djeddah says; then he describes a situation that was precisely Emily's experience. As Emily later learned, James had long wanted to free his highly trained assistant from some of his work in order that the assistant might take on other assignments. When James heard that Emily needed a job, he recollected his own problem. In that moment he created the administrative assistant post, with Emily as its first occupant.

If, as both Jameson and Djeddah emphasize, most jobs are never advertised, how then are they filled? Through personnel departments, through employment agencies, and, yes, definitely through word of mouth by people recommending friends and acquaintances.

Both experts insist that making people aware you are seeking a job is vital. Emily accidentally did this.

Phyllis Boelin did it deliberately. She was at a Little League Football parents' dinner. A man she had seen at community functions over the years was standing next to her. "How's business?" she asked by way of making conversation. "Good. I just hired a new assistant to help me expedite supplies," he answered.

"Really," replied Phyllis. "I would like a job like that. I'm good at scheduling, records, dealing with people."

Her acquaintance paused. "Well," he murmured in empty routine politeness, "I didn't even know you were looking for a job. Maybe next time." They both laughed and let the subject drop. A month later Phyllis was gathering sodden vegetable peels out of the kitchen sink when the phone rang. It was her Little League acquaintance. The person he had hired had not worked out. What exactly was her experience, he wanted to know. She told him. It was prechildren and not that impressive. But he had known her for years as a competent, reliable townsperson. "Tell you the truth, I haven't the strength to start interviewing people all over again. Want to come in and give it a try?" he asked. That was seven years ago. Phyllis is now a company officer.

Phyllis recalls that finding her job was certainly not a fluke. For four months she had been telling people wherever she went that she was looking for a job that would require her to assume responsibility and exercise initiative. Finally, with her present boss, it connected. "On his own, how would he ever have thought of me? He certainly didn't go to an employment agency or advertise the job."

Another woman accompanied her husband to a business dinner. As they chatted with the other couples, who were strangers to them, the auto supply business entered the conversation. One of the men owned four stores. The woman's father had owned a similar store. She added enthusiastically to the discussion, with comments that indicated she had been privy to management's viewpoint. She and the company guest had a pleasant talk on the subject. After dinner, when she implemented her campaign of mentioning that she was in search of a job and asking if they knew of anyone who needed someone reliable and willing to accept responsibility, her auto supply acquaintance came to life. Well, now that she mentioned it, he really needed someone additional to supervise inventory and records, and act as liaison among the stores. Why didn't she stop in the next day, and they could talk about it. (She got the job.) This woman, Doris Koeford, had considered herself a perfect example of "housewife, no marketable skills." Yet someone else saw in her business knowledge that she herself could not perceive. This, combined with the impression she made as a sensible, intelligent woman, caused an employer to invent a job for her. Invented jobs are those for which the need is present, but the employers have not wanted to interview and screen. Like this auto supply owner, they wait for someone "suitable" to "come along." Couldn't you start arranging things so that the someone suitable is you?

You can pleasantly spread the word about your job hunt and then wait to hear what is available (as Phyllis did) or what might be created for you (as Emily and Doris did).

Ask those you meet, "What do you have open in your place? What departments are hiring?" Says Djeddah, most people, even those in high positions, are flattered when you ask their advice. He suggests you ask *for advice, not directly for jobs.* You put it this way: "Do you know someone who might be able to use someone like me? I'm reliable, reasonably intelligent, willing to learn." You are not putting the other person on the spot by asking him to supply you with employment. You are only asking for ideas about which people to approach.

Djeddah explains that you can pyramid this approach. Each person's suggestion leads to others whom you can call or visit with the opening, "John/Jane Doe suggested I call you for *advice* about where I might get a job." Since you are never asking directly for a position, only for advice, Djeddah has learned that each person will seriously think your qualifications through and try to help you. People will do this because in each case you come introduced by a mutual friend and because they are flattered you want their ideas. As people pass you along, each time you have the magic opening, "Peter Jones suggested I make an appointment with you to ask...." Somewhere, as you go along, someone's "advice" will be, "Well, we've been needing someone to take over such and such," and you will have a meaningful job.

Other approaches: Ask friends and acquaintances, "Is anybody quitting at your place? Retiring? Leaving because of a pregnancy or another job? Whom do you suggest I see there? Are there companies that you do business with that are expanding? Hiring?" Salespeople who call on many companies are ideal sources of information about job vacancies and new positions.

The Successful Job-Interview Approach

In all these meetings you are concentrating on what you can offer the employer—your reliability, intelligence, maturity—not on what your employer can do for you. Many people, both women and men, botch their job discussions by wasting valuable time talking about "why I want this job." Face it: The interviewer doesn't give a hoot about your personal dreams or needs! *You will impress an employer best if you concentrate on how your attitude and competencies will be useful in your job.* Western Temporary Services, a nationwide temporary help service with 185 offices, has interviewed hundreds of thousands of job seekers. They suggest that many people fail in an interview for several reasons: (1) They unnecessarily belittle and underrate themselves. (2) They are not flexible enough. They arrive at the meeting with a set idea of the kind of job they want. Though other excellent opportunities are casually suggested by the interviewer, the applicants do not readjust their ideas. They let the other suggestions slide by unheeded. (3) They give the impression that they are "prima donnas." An attitude of "let's try it and see" will take you a lot further. It may even, as Jeanne Vance discovered with her county newspaper ad sales, lead you to a career you enormously enjoy but would never have thought of on your own. Western also has discovered that you strengthen your chances by leaving a complete resume with the interviewer and by being early for the interview. They have found, too, that Monday is better than Friday for results, and morning job meetings go better than afternoon ones.

Once you have the job, do not expect your new boss to work as hard breaking you in and "holding your hand" as your first employer did when you were a youngster fresh out of school. Even though you may be a novice at the kind of work you are doing, the boss and your new co-workers expect you to act in a businesslike and mature manner. (Since you *are* mature and experienced in life, this should be easy.) You can also help yourself by learning the vocabulary of your new occupation as quickly as possible. Recognizing the slang name for a work tool or the business jargon of your new job turns you rapidly from a newcomer into an established member of the work team.

Your Age Is an Asset

Despite the young woman at Emily Menninger's college placement office who thought 46 to be tottering on the lip of the grave, employment specialists often consider older women *more* employable than young women. Says Jameson, " ... being *young* is still the number one barrier for women ... some people consider a woman too young as long as she is capable of bearing children." Though it is illegal for employers to question women on the subject, Jameson suggests that if you have completed your family, you might prejudice the decision in your favor by volunteering this information in your interviews.

Remember as you go about, you are not "unskilled." You are mature, reliable, experienced in life. These are enormously attractive qualities for most employers, especially for those whose jobs are among the 80 percent that are never advertised; and for those who are going to create the three out of ten jobs when someone "suitable" appears.

2

From "No Skills" to Your "Ideal" Job

While researching this book, I often heard women say, "Well, since I can't do the kind of work I really want to do, I guess I'll have to settle for a nothing job. At least it'll give me something to do every day and some money."

When I ask, "What is it you would really like to do?" the answers are varied. "I'd really like to be in fashion; work for some important social cause; work with something in medicine; and so on. Every woman has her own reply, including the myriad of women who say, "I want something interesting, but I don't know what."

When the woman who wants the fashion or social cause or medical occupation is asked if she has ever tried to get a job like that, she frequently looks startled. No, she admits, she has never made the smallest effort toward the job or career she regards as her ideal. Yet she has already resigned herself: "Since I can't work at what I'd really like most, I'll take whatever comes along."

If she has never made the simplest attempt to enter her chosen field, how then can she be so sure it is beyond her reach?

We are not discussing occupations like lawyer or doctor or architect, where there are years of study between you and the occupation. We are talking about the easily accessible: for example, fashion, work for a social cause, even certain kinds of medical careers, all of which you can enter quickly by using your life experience and inventiveness.

Having No Skills Can Be an Asset

Turn your lack of skills around, and view it as an asset instead of a problem. The woman who is a trained accountant or teacher or stenographer or nurse may feel herself locked into a profession she has outgrown. At 17 or 18, when she was young and unformed, she chose that vocation. Now that she has the skill, it offers her work at a good salary. She or her family may not think it is "sensible" for her to go skylarking off after new training for her grown-up interests. But you, because you have "no skills," are as free as a youngster to follow your desires. You can seek a job anywhere. Why not choose exactly the milieu that offers you pride in achievement and the social and emotional satisfactions you want? Is it really all that difficult? Adele Lerner, with her one year of college and "no skills," sat down with the telephone book business pages when she decided she wanted a career "helping people in a social agency." A few weeks later, as we discussed in Section II, after only five phone calls, she had two impressive offers from the United Fund and the Heart Fund.

The telephone book can be put to similar use for every sort of aspiration. In this chapter we will suggest numerous other approaches toward inventing exactly the job you want.

First, it is necessary to know what you want. Some women can focus on a specific occupation: interior decorating, journalism, fashion. Yet an enormous number of women with "no skills" are paralyzed because they cannot think their way through to a specific answer. They are the ones who say, "I want something interesting, but I don't know what."

If you are one of these women, you may be able to solve your dilemma and produce an answer if you stop thinking about which occupation you want and begin asking, "What do I want the job to do for my lifestyle?"

I Want Something Interesting, But I Don't Know What

When industrial psychologists conducted an experiment on work goals, they discovered that most people in the study wildly misunderstood why people work. "Money, first, second, and last. What else?" was the most popular answer. Yet, in the same experiment, when people were asked what they would do about their jobs if they suddenly inherited a lifetime income, almost 70 percent of the white collar workers and 65 percent of the factory workers were horrified at the idea of quitting their jobs. "I'd miss the social contacts with people all day. Besides I'd be bored crazy," was the general attitude.

In thinking about the kind of job you would enjoy, if you have been concentrating only on such practical aspects as income, the prestige of the occupation, and the training required, you may have been approaching your particular need from the wrong side. That may be why you have not been able to satisfy it.

For the moment, forget about pinpointing a specific occupation. Think of what is missing from your life, what emotional and social benefits you are hungry for that the job might provide for you. My friend, Rita Gannon, who moved to California with her family several years ago, successfully analyzed her problem by that method. She has taken a rather routine office job in her new community, but she "loves it."

Why?

"It's just what I need at this stage of my life." Rita explains that in a new community it was difficult for a post-35-year-old woman to make friends. "Once your children pass the primary grades, they're not the natural contact point for adults, and it's often hard to break into established neighborhood groups." More self-aware and analytical than most people, she realized that she yearned for heavy social contacts on her job. She refused an administrative job at high pay in a one-person office. "It would have been perfect for someone who was after responsibility and a chance for initiative and advancement. But it didn't have what I needed." Rita searched instead for a large business with many women in the office and company-sponsored sports and social events. Once Rita thought through *what she wanted the job to do for her lifestyle,* she was able to look for and locate the right kind of position.

Even without the upheaval of moving, many women find that by their mid-30s, 40s, or 50s their social lives have stagnated. There are contacts with a few friends and too many empty lonely hours and days in between. A job where you work daily with other people can lead you easily into a new social group and new friendships. Perhaps what you have been thinking of as an "interesting" job really translates into "a job that will allow me to be with people all day and where I'll find a new social life during and after working hours."

If you discover that this is true of you, you can stop tormenting yourself trying to decide on a specific industry. Your answer is *not* a specific occupation but rather a specific *type* of work, a job offering many co-workers and the opportunity to deal with people. Almost *any* job that fits that definition will give you the social contacts you desire, and will therefore be the "interesting" work you have been hoping for.

Other women may find that once they begin thinking of what they want the job to do for their lives, they realize that all their hesitation and indecision were protective devices to prevent them from finding a job. When they think the problem through, these women discover they do not really want to have to get up every morning, get dressed, and go off to work. Though they are bored and dissatisfied, what they genuinely want is to continue the activities they have so enjoyed during their years as homemakers and mothers. Women sometimes temporarily solve this problem by having that one last baby. But even the last baby grows up. Then what?

If you realize that what you truly desire is to continue your at-home, child-centered routines, your life experience has prepared you superbly to invent a career. It can be as small or as large as you wish. You are in total control. All the other middle-class women in your neighborhood who are rushing out to careers and colleges are searching frantically for you.

You can therefore tailor your career to your precise taste. Do you most enjoy elementary school children? Do you recall with most pleasure the hours after school from three to dinnertime when they used to come home eager for a snack and play? Fifty-one percent of all women with children living at home now work. One-fourth of all children now live in one-parent homes, homes broken by divorce, separation, death. Nearly a third of mothers of preschool children now work. That adds up to a lot of middle-class children right in your own neighborhood who need a "mother" to come home to after school. From three to six o'clock every weekday you can be that paid "mother" in *your* home.

The number of children you accept is completely up to you. Let it be known you are available (use the methods Carole Arund used to publicize her home version of Music Time), and you will soon have a long waiting list. How can you doubt it? Wouldn't you have been ecstatic when your children were young if you had been able to find in your neighborhood a warm, reliable woman like you to see to your children when you were not available?

Not only will such work give you full, busy days and children in your home, but it also will automatically increase your friendships and social life among all the parent neighbors you are in daily contact with.

Or perhaps you most enjoyed the little ones. Again, in your own family room or playroom you can open a neighborhood day care center or nursery school, whichever you prefer. When my daughter was two, my husband was offered an industrial consulting contract in Israel. For the year we lived there, I never stopped marveling at how glorious the day care for toddlers was. There were few blocks in our middle-class suburb that lacked a nursery school. Each of these schools was run by a neighborhood woman who enjoyed children and had bought some good secondhand toys; presto! she was in business. Every mother had a nursery school within easy strolling distance from her home, and the teacher was a neighbor. It was a delight. Some women accepted only four to five children. Some joined with a friend or neighbor as business partner, and the two together accepted as many as ten or fifteen children for a morning.

I have checked legal requirements with the Cooperative Child Care Council, a group funded to develop day-care facilities for American children. Many states have *no laws,* so you may take as many children as you and your partners think sensible. Even states that do have pertinent laws usually allow a woman to take as many as five children into her home for nursery school or day care without any to-do over license, zoning, or other legal requirements. You can look into the matter with your state department of education.

Nursery schools can be easy to set up. Many states require no teacher training for those in charge. If your state does ask for teaching credentials for nursery school (which are different from those for day care, and more stringent sometimes), there is such a glut of unemployed teachers that you will be able to hire one as your partner and thereby fullfill the requirement.

How many hours a day should you work? Remember, you are in total command. You are inventing this career. Do you want to work only a few hours? In the morning? In the afternoon? All day? Some nursery schools operate only for two and a half hours in the morning; some only two to three hours during the early afternoon. Some accept two groups—one in the morning, one in the afternoon. Some are day-care operations from eight till five. Choose the arrangment that will give you the kind of daily life you will enjoy.

Would you like to invent this career on a large scale? One woman in Wisconsin began with five children in her home and now runs a four-woman partnership with 80 children (40 in the morning, 40 in the afternoon). They have rented space from a church. You could do the same if you have a mind to.

Perhaps you want to work with children but not in the above forms. There are many possible variations. When Betty Friedan was writing *The Feminine Mystique,* she had three young children of her own. To fulfill her weekly car-pool obligations, she hired a taxi. She reports that the other mothers, being preliberation full-time mommies, were outraged. Today, in the liberated world *The Feminine Mystique* wrought, career-minded mommies in your neighborhood will happily line up to hire you if you offer to operate an after-school service chauffeuring their children to scouts, music lessons, dentist, dance lessons, religious school instruction—well, you know the list.

When You Know What You Would Love to Do

When you have no skills but do know what occupation you would enjoy, for heaven's sake, before you decide, "Since I can't do the work I want . . .," try. Shades of Horatio Alger and all that. Onward and Upward, and Success May Be Waiting. It sounds corny, but the truth is that with very little effort you may snare your own version of a "dream job" by straightforwardly going after it.

During the year I was writing this book in addition to doing formal research, everywhere I went I talked to people about their experiences. At a party I met a young woman who had invented an interesting direct approach. She was still in her twenties, very much house-bound, with young children. As so many people are these days, she had become passionately involved with plants. So frequent a visitor was she at her neighborhood plant store—buying, browsing, obtaining information—that eventually she and the 55-year-old woman who owned the store became friends. "I told her I'd like to help her. I hired a sitter two afternoons a week and worked for her for free. I read piles of books about plants, learned a lot. When people brought in their sick plants, I learned to accurately diagnose and prescribe for them. Now I'm a plant doctor and I make house calls."

I stopped eating my canape. "A plant doctor? House calls?"

"I'm paid twenty dollars a house call. I have a microscope and a traveling medical kit of plant medications. I also lecture for women's groups and community groups at seventy-five dollars a lecture. It just grew out of the shop. People used to call and want someone to come see their sick plants. I started doing it."

If you'll excuse the pun, by planting herself firmly in the plant store, she had invented her "dream" job.

The owner of the plant business had also invented her career. When her children grew up, she "didn't have a skill and didn't know what to do with herself." She had always worked with plants as a hobby. Someone said to her, "You're so good at it. Why don't you open a plant store?" (To see yourself as others see you.) Using her own plants as her original stock, she began selling from her home, then plowed the money back, eventually rented a store, and now has expanded to plant landscaping indoors and outdoors.

More Ways to Invent the Career You Want

Another woman created the jewelry-merchandising career she wanted by pleasantly asking about part-time work in a few town jewelry stores. She didn't volunteer to work free, as the plant woman had, but merely told each owner she lived in the area and then left her name and address with him. While she was standing there before him, the owner could appraise her demeanor, manner of dress, speech, and the ability she projected. Several weeks later, when the fall holiday rush began, two owners called her. She chose one and worked till the end of January. Her employer called her again in the spring. For three years thereafter, she worked year round except for layoffs in quiet summer months, a part-time arrangement perfectly matched to her children's school vacation. Her children are in their teens now and she has taken her in-depth experience as general factotum in a small jewelry store to a nearby high-fashion department store. There she is manager of the jewelry department.

For another woman, her "ideal" job meant a fabric and crafts store of her own someday. Lacking any retail knowledge, she decided to acquire the necessary information before investing. Adele Lerner used the phone book to track down an abstraction: "a job where I can help people in a health organization." This woman used the same telephone business pages to locate a practical, mercantile job. She called fabric and crafts stores throughout her area, asking if they needed part-time help. On her twenty-third call (only three days later) the owner said, yes, more part-time help would free her to offer additional crafts demonstrations and talks to women's groups, which generated store business. Again, a job was created when someone proffered her services.

An employer can know for a long time that he or she needs additional help but may hesitate to take on the headaches of advertising a job and then sifting through an avalanche of applicants. When you seek out an employer on your own, you are voluntarily expressing an interest in that occupation. It makes you seem well suited, simpatico. Since the job is unadvertised, perhaps not even invented, you are the only candidate. Is it surprising that you often secure the job? Then your abilities and skill increase as you work. The woman in the crafts store says she is learning wholesale markets, buying, retail advertising, store display, retail rent, and utility costs—everything she needs to know. "Another year, and I'll be ready to open my store in a neighboring town."

Sometimes It Takes a Little Effort

Mildred Cassidy had a different kind of no-skill problem. She had always been fascinated by things medical and wanted to become a medical secretary. She located an adult school that offered medical terminology. (A different use of the adult school from our past examples—this time from the pupil's viewpoint, as the speedy gateway to the career knowledge you need.) Then she struck a dead end. She mastered the terminology, but nowhere in her area could she locate an adult school, community college, or secretarial school that offered medical transcription training. Medical transcription, like legal stenography, is a well-paid specialty. Besides, it intrigued Mildred. She could have shrugged her shoulders, murmured, "Well, if I can't do the work . . . ," and accepted a routine secretarial job.

Instead she made one more phone call. She called the instructor of her town adult school, who had taught the terminology course and asked advice. "You could come in as a volunteer and work with me at the hospital," the instructor said. "I'll train you." Mildred had been ready to pay for training. Three months later, by volunteering to help someone who had the skill, Mildred knew what she needed to know to apply for a job of her own.

Though the first ad she answered asked for a full-time commitment, Mildred stumbled on an additional way to locate part-time work. When she phoned, she asked if there were any possibility of arranging part-time hours. She says there was a strange pause on the other end of the wire, and the voice responded in surprise, "As a matter of fact, all we really need is someone extra for three days a week. It never occurred to us to make it part-time. We were going to search for odds and ends to fill the other two days."

Would volunteering to help someone who has the skill you are interested in solve your problem? You can learn many skills rapidly when you are a volunteer because you are working as one pupil with the undivided teaching attention of your mentor. It is a near-perfect learning situation, another excellent way to go from "no skill" to your ideal job.

Unless you make an attempt, how will you ever know whether or not your job or career idea is within your reach? Wouldn't it be a pity if it were easily available to you, and you didn't bother to put out your hand?

3
When Your Skills
Are Too Rusty

If you met them, they would seem like four very different kinds of women. Yet they had the same problem. Renee Florain is an experienced medical laboratory technician; Bernadine Riebling used to teach fourth grade; Sylvia Evans spent six years as a psychiatric social worker (B.A, M.S.W.); and Eleanor Stern was a pioneer. Twenty years ago Eleanor breached the feminine job stereotypes, became an electrical engineer, and worked at her profession for four years before settling in as a full-time mother and homemaker. Though their occupations and personalities are very dissimilar, Renee, Bernadine, Sylvia, and Eleanor shared the same dilemma. They were all afraid to return to their old occupations.

They worried: Is my basic knowledge obsolete? Have my professional skills rusted away? Can I catch up? At my age, can I succeed with studying if I have to? Would anyone give me a job, considering how many years I've been home?

To complete their emotional turmoil, in the back of their minds hovered their worst fantasy: They get their courage up and go job hunting. Mirabile dictu, someone does offer them a job. There they are at work the first few weeks, nakedly unable to cope, stumbling flat on their faces.

Because her predicament involves many fears, the woman whose skills are rusty often spends months, even years, in vacillating indecision. She is reluctant to jettison a profession she has trained for, yet is unsure of her ability to return to it. What to do?

Sylvia Evans told me, "Besides my fears about my skills being obsolete, I really didn't know if I wanted to be a social worker again." She explained her attitude in words that millions of over-30 American women would recognize.

"My parents sent me to college and drummed into me the idea that my profession was a kind of insurance policy. When I married, in case my husband was sick or, God forbid, died or couldn't make a living, then I'd be prepared. Never any idea of my having a career for itself. Working was merely something I did till I married and had children. With that outlook, the whole six years I worked, I was dissatisfied. I didn't enjoy it. My mind was on finding the right man and getting married.

"So, not only was I fearful about being able to handle the work after all these years, I didn't even know if I wanted it. I hadn't liked it very much."

Sylvia's youngest child was in nursery school. As with so many people, an additional family income was an attractive idea. She hesitated for almost a year. She experimented with substitute teaching. Not for her. She enrolled in a stock-market brokerage course. No, not for her. "I was much too insecure about my sixteen years away from the profession to dream of applying for a social work job. Mostly, I went on being a homemaker and revolving the problem round and round in my mind."

At last she decided that, with all the years she had invested in college degrees and work experience, she ought at least to test social work possibilities. She volunteered one day a week at a mental health clinic.

For Sylvia, volunteering within her profession dissolved all her rusty-skills fears. "As soon as I sat down and interviewed my first patient, I knew I was all right. I was flooded with a feeling of 'I'm O.K. This is for me. I'm in the right place.' I don't mean I was instantly perfect, but I knew immediately, after all my doubts, that I really was suited to social work. I quickly discovered the new grown-up me liked it very much."

Instead of being handicapped by the years of motherhood and life at home, Sylvia realized that the years were an undiluted asset. "I understood people and the human relations problems I was counseling people on vastly better than any young adult ever could." This would be true of teaching, nursing, and any other profession that is people-oriented; you would find that your life experience has inevitably enriched your perceptions and hence your ability.

Sylvia recommends volunteering as a possible solution for others. "The important thing is somehow to get your feet wet; try it out, and see whether you really have significant reentry problems or whether you are just nervous. If a woman has the confidence to jobhunt immediately in her old occupation, then, of course, she can skip volunteering," says Sylvia. "But even when I discovered I liked it, I lacked that confidence."

Sylvia updated her knowledge and skill during the year that she volunteered (one or two days weekly). She read a few books; absorbed information at staff meetings, professional organization talks, and seminars; and consulted with supervisors when she came upon a puzzling situation. As she met other social workers, she compared her knowledge with theirs and gained confidence as she realized she measured up. The results she saw among those she counseled, however, were her most powerful encouragement.

"Would you like a paid job? Someone I know is looking for additional staff," the director asked her. His willingness to recommend her further strengthened her assurance. The convenient three-day-a-week job she now holds was the result of his recommendation. "Being there as a volunteer, I had my foot in the door when opportunity arose." (Volunteering also works in the current skimpy teachers' job market. A number of people I interviewed told me of teachers they know who, unable to find jobs, volunteered as teacher's aides in their neighborhood schools. Thus, whenever a teacher resigned in mid-term because of a health problem, pregnancy, or other reason, a teacher's aide was always available, knew the school, knew the children, and the principal eagerly asked her if she would "please" accept the appointment.) Sylvia also feels volunteering gave her the transition period necessary to learn how to juggle home and job without the pressures of being formally employed.

Four years after she began as an apprehensive volunteer, Sylvia is not only calmly managing home, three children, and a part-time job, but she also is leading a workshop for parents at a large community college, and she is in demand through her county

Mental Health Association for paid talks and for workshop sessions at P.T.A. and women's group meetings.

Can You Really Catch Up?

Sylvia's success as psychiatric social worker, speaker, and college teacher attests to how well she has caught up. Others can do as well in their professions. The more people-oriented and the less technical your skill is, the less effort you will probably have to expend. Sciences change; people do not.

Since you were probably channeled into one of the traditional women's professions (teaching, nursing, library work), all of which are people-oriented, you probably have few, if any, courses to take. Like Sylvia, you may be able to learn to operate the new machines, speak the new jargon, and adapt to the new techniques after only a short interval on the job. Or perhaps going through a few current books in your field is all the renewal you will need. When Renee Florain investigated her profession of medical laboratory technician, she realized it had grown *easier.* Machines now do the blood counts and mathematics she used to have to compute. "I'd have to learn to operate the new devices, but the work really is much simpler."

Probably only the sciences, engineering, law, medicine, and other such technical occupations, will require considerable classroom updating, *unless you sidestep the problem by devising a way to move around it.*

As a design engineer, Eleanor Stern has found that her skills are not only rusty, but also obsolete. Such is the speed of engineering developments that many of Eleanor's male classmates find themselves in the same predicament. Even those men who have worked at their profession and struggled to stay abreast through professional journals frequently find themselves by age 40 to 45 overwhelmed by new developments and elbowed aside by fresh graduates brimful of the newest information. Eleanor can do what these men do: move sideways in her profession. She can obtain a staff engineering position where her engineering background is necessary to coordinate projects, keep track of project expenditures, see that schedules are kept, and correlate and analyze reports. Thus, a recently graduated current engineer will not be "wasted" on these non-design projects. Yet an engineer's training is necessary to hold down such a job. Eleanor can, with a smattering of refresher courses, do the work.

Or if she has the personality, she can become a sales engineer. In the chapter on Heidi Friedman and selling, we mentioned the male sales electrical engineer whose drawing-board skills are as dated as Eleanor's. So he uses his engineering knowledge to understand the products he sells and his customers' needs. Eleanor can do the same. She can also apply her skills outside her profession. Though there is a general surplus of teachers, there is still an insufficient number of high school math teachers. Too rusty to be a practicing engineer, Eleanor is certainly still capable of explaining high school algebra, trigonometry, and geometry.

This pattern of taking professional skills into staff, administrative, or sales positions in the same profession or into related jobs on the periphery, such as high school or community college math or science teaching, would also be the solution for other women whose skills are technologically outmoded.

But Who Will Hire You?

Lots of people will. The media may prate about employers' yen for youth. Privately many employers have arrived at diametrically opposite conclusions. A hospital research lab director (a middle-aged male) put it to me unequivocally. "I'd much rather hire a middle-aged woman as a lab technician and spend three months retraining her if she's been out of the field than hire a young woman or young man who is already trained.

"I know the middle-aged woman wants the job, or she wouldn't be there. She'll feel an obligation to the job, be reliable. The young ones are there because they need something to fill their time, and they need spending money. Seldom any real job commitment."

It sounded great. Yet he had not mentioned the albatross that is always thought to weigh down the jobholder who is also a mother. "Aren't you worried about the woman's being out because her children are sick or for family obligations?"

He laughed. "The young ones are out much more. They call in

sick to go swimming, skiing, shopping, because they're hung over from a late date. ... They quit to move to another state, get married, try another type of work—you name it. The older woman is much more reliable."

A recent in-depth study of American working women by the huge Esmark Corporation confirmed the hospital director's private observations. The study reported that 14,481,000 American working women were 40 years or older and that employers had found that "older is better; older women are more dependable workers."

In short, employers in every occupation have observed the same patterns and developed the same attitudes. They will be pleased to see you.

The Put-Down Interview

While she was job hunting, Sylvia noticed two kinds of interviewers the "rusty" job seeker might meet. One was interested in appraising the candidate's knowledge, maturity, potential. "I did well with them despite my having been out of the field for so long," says Sylvia. Then there was the put-down interviewer. You can protect yourself from discouragement by realizing you may meet a few of them. One man cross-examined Sylvia about the latest social work techniques. When she admitted she didn't know what they were, he lashed into her. "How do you expect to get a job? Who do you think will hire you if you're not up on the latest methods?" He brought to life all the worst nightmares of homemakers struggling to overcome self-doubt. Says Sylvia, "Fortunately, I had already had other interviews where I was well received, so this experience didn't panic me. If it had been my first, I might have been crushed and never dared try again. The funny thing was the man who chewed me out was offering much less money and a less important job than the one I was eventually presented with."

If you do meet any of these put-down sadists, realize that they are the exceptions. Shrug and move on to a better job, where they will see your maturity as a plus and your slightly dated skills as a minor flaw that can quickly be remedied.

Yes, But Suppose You Do Have to Take Courses?

Women in their 30s, 40s, 50s, 60s, and older are jamming college classrooms because they either have to or want to and are succeeding. According to the latest Census Bureau statistics, nearly half a million women over 35 have enrolled in college either as freshmen (freshwomen) or as more advanced students continuing their studies. Most do supremely well. Laura O. Kornfield, who heads the Academic Advisory Center for Adults, reports, "Every dean I've ever talked with is enthralled with older students. They say the mature ones are so smart, so industrious, and so eager." George Washington University checked its older women students' grades and found that 81 percent of them were earning either *As* or *Bs*. The Educational Testing Service (E.T.S.) of Princeton, New Jersey (the people who create and administer the college entrance examinations) undertook a special research project on the older student and discovered that they have fewer academic problems than younger college people. The E.T.S. comments, "Perhaps the older students' experience in work and home life has given them a realistic picture of their talents, physical stamina, and mental capacities."

Creating Your Own Happiness

We had switched off the tape recorder and were coffee klatching when Sylvia paused. "The most important thing I've gotten from my job . . .," she said. I punched the "on" button.

"I had grown up to feel you do things for others, and this is where you get your happiness. You do things for your family, and this brings you happiness. When you get married, you do things for your husband and children, and they bring you happiness. I never learned till I went back to work that working to me meant I brought myself my own happiness. Myself.

"This was something I was doing. I wasn't dependent upon other people to bring me, to give me, happiness I was looking for.

"I as an individual had an entity of my own. And *this* part was the most important part to working. Do you understand what I mean?"

"The discovery?"

"Yes, the discovery that I didn't *have to be dependent,* waiting for someone else to come home to bring me satisfaction. Waiting constantly for someone else. I myself was capable of it.

"A tremendous, tremendous thing to me."

A long journey of discovery to have taken in only four years, from wondering if she wanted to work and if anyone wanted her.

Sylvia's discovery, of course, is precisely what the women's movement is all about: loving others but not attempting to live *through* them. Yet I had never heard its effect on a woman's life explained so clearly.

SECTION VIII

YOUR "IMPOSSIBLE DREAM": A BUSINESS OF YOUR OWN

1
Controlling Success and Failure in Your New Business

Probably the quintessential American Dream, masculine-style, has always meant owning a piece of the action, a business of your own. Now, as women enter the mainstream of American life, many are daring to dream The Dream. Perhaps you are one of them. When you allow your mind's eye to focus, what do you see? A retail store? Ownership of a service organization, such as a real estate business, travel bureau, employment agency, public relations firm, secretarial employment agency? A business you can run from your home? A life as a free-lance artist or as a proprietor of an art gallery? A manufacturing company?

The New England office of the United States Small Business Administration reports that in 1976 women occupied 50 percent of the seats at their Going into Business for Yourself workshops, a huge increase from 15 percent in 1975. Major insurance companies, which never squander their advertising dollars, have discovered a new market and have taken to running large ads directed at "the American Businesswoman . . . to insure her life, her home, her *company* [emphasis added]. . . ."

There have always been some women who have owned businesses, but they were the exceptions. Today, women who own businesses are part of a trend. Says John Seely of the Phoenix Small Business Administration office, "We're seeing an increase in women owners and also an increase in partnership situations where women are much more active in management decisions."

Women Entrepreneurs: Some Advantages

The woman who hopes to own a business has two, and sometimes three, advantages over a man. No, it's not all Pollyanna. Despite the non-discrimination laws, women may still have sex-related problems obtaining financing. But first let's cheer ourselves with the plusses. Fifty percent of all new businesses fail within the first year. The causes are varied, and we'll come to them. But one of the commonest causes is insufficient money. Call it by any of its financial names, "undercapitalization," "tight money flow," "inability to meet operating expenses," it all comes down to the business's failure to generate enough money *both* to support the owner's family and also operate the business.

If a woman is married and is being supported by her husband, she has the precious opportunity to run the business for that treacherous first year, and even longer if necessary, without draining money from it. In all fairness, it must be pointed out that some men have successfully developed businesses by reversing the situation, i.e. living from a wife's job earnings until his company prospered.

In Section VI we discussed Johnson O'Connor research discoveries about women's and men's career aptitudes. Aptitudes must be complemented by the required personality traits in order to succeed in an occupation. You might have the high idea flow that a commission salesperson needs, but you might prefer solitude to people. You would have the aptitude but not the personality. Similarly, to succeed as an entrepreneur, you need certain personality traits. Here we come to a woman's second asset. Says Dr. Arthur A. Witkin, chief psychologist for Personnel Sciences Center in New York, which has helped employers select 50,000 employees for hiring or promotion since 1948, "There is only one personality factor that separates executive and entrepreneur women from their male counterparts—and in this factor women are generally superior."

Contrary to the antiwomen myths, Dr. Witkin explains that this superior quality is "independence; this includes the ability to make a decision without a committee to support it, an emotional detachment that enables the person to see herself/himself and surroundings objectively, assertiveness, and the ability to react to criticism without undue sensitivity. On the average," he continues, "women rank higher in these areas than males who are on their employment level, based on our psychological test results, evaluations during personal interviews, and the experience of employees who come to us for career counseling. It's a kind of Darwinian survival. In our business world, women would never survive to become entrepreneurs or supervisors if they didn't have emotional detachment, independence, assertiveness, etc."

The woman business owner's third potential advantage lies in the reverse side of the mocking, "Can a woman really run a business?" Many women business owners have made a pleasant discovery. As an owner of an Oregon public relations firm wrote me, "As soon as I did a couple of jobs well, the word-of-mouth recommendation was powerful. The fact that I was a woman competently heading a business made me very visible. I wasn't 'just another O.K. company,' I was 'that company owned by a woman which does a good job.' I stood out in people's and potential customers' minds. True there are some accounts I can never seem to land. But if I were a man in business, there would be some accounts which for various reasons I was never able to land. Overall, the visibility has been an advantage."

Why Businesses Succeed, Why They Fail

So, fine, you have all these strengths. What do you do now? Just seize your "impossible dream," and rush into business with it? "No, no, no," warns Dr. Emanuel Orlick, a man who probably knows as much or more than anyone about success and failure factors in new businesses. Combining a career of scholarship with 10 years of independent, active work in the management consultant business and another ten years of casework supervision for the United States Small Business Administration, Dr. Orlick has concentrated on causes of new business success and failure. During these years, Dr. Orlick's programs and knowledge have been recognized with a variety of regional and national citations. He told me, "I own hundreds of books that deal with business success and failure, copies of every survey that's been done on the subject, my own surveys, all added to my years of practical experience. Your preparation and knowledge before you open your business can make the complete difference in your results!"

Dr. Orlick continues, "Besides the fifty percent of businesses that fail in the first year, another twenty-five percent fail in their second, another ten percent in the third, five percent in the fourth. Only one out of ten businesses which start each year is functioning five years later. Yet *the success ratio could be much higher if people would only observe some sensible guidelines.*

"Going into business is like marriage. It's one of the biggest things you'll ever do in your life, and, like marriage, people rush into it without knowledge or sufficient forethought. You wouldn't go out to steer a new motorboat without taking some instruction. You wouldn't even begin to play golf without asking a few procedure questions. Yet people invest their life savings, their credit standing, their strength, their own lives, and the future of their families in businesses without doing the most elementary kind of planning.

"There are always enough tales around to mislead neophytes about someone now flourishing who started a business on a shoestring. If you probe, you discover that behind the 'miracle' tale lies adherence to the necessary business success patterns. Some rare people may have a natural business sense and do things right by instinct. But counting on being a born business mastermind is what puts so many people into the ninety percent failure class. Better to observe some proven business wisdoms and ease gracefully into the success group."

I told Dr. Orlick about Nancy De Vries, whom I had interviewed. Nancy, with her partner, Lynda Thomas, had started a typesetting business ten years before. The firm was thriving. As Nancy had told it to me, it had seemed that she and Lynda had just drifted into it, found customers, and continued growing year by year. Yet as I listened to myself retelling their story, I realized that Nancy DeVries and Lynda Thomas had in truth done it by the book. Through intelligence *and the necessary previous experience,* they had done it right step by step, according to the basic guidelines Dr. Orlick had just outlined to me. Dr. Orlick was openly impressed. "They seem to have done things right," he agreed.

Step by Step

Yet Nancy had told me when I interviewed her in her hilltop suburban home, "Lynda and I started ten years ago, way before the women's movement had affected people's thinking. We didn't really have any great goals. No real plan. We had met at a P.T.A., known each other for three years. We both had three children. My youngest child was in kindergarten; hers was going in the fall. We weren't the kind of people who want to sit and drink coffee and just talk. Lynda had had two years of college as an English major. I had one year. Then we both got married and had children.

"My husband owns a successful printing business, and one day he asked us if we'd like to do a fairly simple, one-shot job he'd heard of. You know those trading stamp companies that give you all kinds of premiums when you've saved enough stamps. One of them wanted to eliminate an item from their catalogue. They needed someone to open one *million* catalogues, apply a silk screen patch by hand to blot out that item, then repack the catalogues in cartons. A million catalogues, we found out, is three garages full. Floor to ceiling, front to back. We grabbed our kids, got them to help after school, hired some housewife friends. It was hard work, but fun.

"Then we contracted with a printing company to collate and do bindery work that could be done at Lynda's and my home. I'd once worked in a bindery and I'd done silk screening in school, making Xmas cards and selling them. Lynda's husband at that time was in advertising, buying print communications. So Lynda, naturally, had absorbed the terminology of the print industry from listening to him. We did the collating for nine months, hiring housewives when we were very busy, working out of our recreation rooms. We were learning to manage our time, employees, business priorities.

"Next, through my husband we heard about a new kind of typesetting machine that IBM had that could be leased for $150 a month." Of course, other women might have listened to the IBM information and never used it. Nancy and Lynda hurried out and rented a machine and began cold canvassing of printers offering to prepare copy for them.

"In the beginning, we made mistakes. We'd often feel inferior. We had no experience and we would be talking to people who were very experienced. But we knew what the going rates were, and we asked less; we didn't have the rent overhead, and we didn't have to give ourselves big salaries." °

Perhaps all of Nancy's and Lynda's experiences so far sound like an accident or good fortune. After all, Nancy had worked in a bindery. Her husband and Lynda's were in the graphic arts field. They had information readily accessible. Could they have succeeded without these family connections?

"It doesn't matter where you get the background information," says Dr. Orlick. "Family, personal working experience of your own, friends, but in one way or another it is an *absolute necessity!* All things being equal, your chances of business success rise with every bit of previous knowledge and experience you have of that particular business. One of the major causes of business failure is insufficient knowledge of that occupation. This ignorance leads people into actions which are grossly incompetent. Dun & Bradstreet estimates that 'incompetence' plus 'lack of experience in line' account for fifty-two percent of all failures."

In order to price, to find customers, to recognize an opportunity (for example, that the new I.B.M. machine could be used to solicit typesetting business from printers), you must have previous knowledge and understanding of your prospective enterprise. And by working in the bindery, Nancy had invoked a basic business success maxim: Let someone else pay for your apprenticeship. Says Dr. Orlick, "You can learn more in one month of work at a successful concern of the type that interests you than you can in two years of blundering on your own. More important, your

---

° Dr. Orlick did mention that this was the only place where they might have encountered difficulties. If they had trespassed on union rates with their price scale, they might have aroused union hostility against them. This did not happen.

In a follow-up discussion, Nancy commented, "'The kind of typesetting which we do is called 'cold composition' and as such is not covered by the A.L.A. [American Lithographers Association] or any other printing trade unons."

However, if the business you are thinking of entering is covered by labor organizations, it would be worthwhile to keep Dr. Orlick's suggestions in mind.

working experience will save you from all kinds of expensive and often fatal errors. You'll start out knowing how to do it right. In the end it will save you money. It's also possible you may discover that once inside that occupation, it doesn't appeal to you. This is a very common occurrence. Isn't it better to find that out before you invest your life savings?"

Nancy and Lynda enjoyed their work. "But it was hectic," Nancy remembers. "Our children were young. After school there'd be six children in the recreation room playing and watching T.V. while we worked. A client would call, and we'd be trying to sound very businesslike with a T.V. Mickey Mouse booming in the background." A blonde, tall, pretty woman ("when I was first married, I gave Tupperware parties to earn money for modeling lessons"), Nancy laughed as she remembered those scenes.

As they went along, the partners realized that various accounts were eluding them because the printers would sometimes have trouble laying out their typeset pages. Printers had to cut the typeset pages apart, insert headlines and art work, and set the whole in the needed design. Sometimes printers smeared or damaged the typeset portions in some way. The women decided they had to learn to paste up. "If we could offer customers work not only typeset but pasted-up as was needed, then we'd have added a service they wanted."

The successful company, Dr. Orlick had explained, must first be adapted to meet a current need at a competitive price (for example, setting type for printers); and then be alert and adaptable enough to grow as new needs become evident (adding the paste-up service). Without these two characteristics, there are no customers and no business. For example, just opening a retail store, he pointed out, is foolish till you have ascertained if (1) there is a need for this product, (2) at these prices, (3) in this area.

"So we bought a drawing board, a T-square, a pot of rubber cement. No, it never occurred to us that we couldn't learn. We were poor typists and had to work hard to master the I.B.M. machine, and in the paste-up we made mistakes, too. We'd be told, 'This is wrong. Do it again.' Also lots of doing and redoing over and over and over because we ourselves weren't satisfied.

"I remember once our having worked till four in the morning

in Lynda's rec room and my sneaking out of Lynda's house so as not to wake her husband and sneaking into my house so as not to wake my husband. They would have been very upset with us. But we were determined to make it go. We didn't know where we were going. But we wanted to do what we did well."

With just the $150-a-month expense for machine rental, they had neutralized the crucial cash-flow problem. Nine months after they first rented the machine, they signed a publishing contract for book typesetting that was so huge it forced a move from their homes to office space. To make the move and take on additional computerized typesetting equipment, they applied to a local bank with a reputation for supporting small businesses. They asked for a $3,000 loan. "We could have used family money, but we were determined to do it on our own."

The banker told them, "We think three thousand dollars is insufficient. We'll give you four thousand dollars."

"To us, in those days, that was an immense amount of money. And for an unsecured loan besides."

Luck? No, not at all.

Madeline McWhinney, former president of the new First Women's Bank in New York, has commented that the increasing number of requests for business loans that her bank receives reflects a fundamental business misconception.

"Many of those loans are not bankable loans because what they are seeking is equity capital. They have to get started from their own sources, and we can help with working capital," she said. "This need to show a bank at least a kernel of investment before asking for a loan is something many persons going into a small business, of either sex, do not realize." With more than a year of successful performance behind them and a big contract in their pocket, there was nothing lucky about Nancy's and Lynda's loan episode. They had abundantly met the banking industry's loan criteria.

They rented one floor of a local building and retained a lawyer to draw up a partnership agreement and an accountant to show them how to keep their books. They had already contacted an insurance agent for workers' accident compensation when they were hiring housewives for at-home work. ("Remarkable," said Dr. Orlick with obvious respect when I mentioned this to him.)

The accountant explained the various employee government withholding regulations. "There are tables for everything. You don't have to figure it out yourself. There's nothing to it," says Nancy. "Till we got too big and busy, we always did our own payroll and books."

Businesses get into all kinds of difficulties and often find themselves abruptly padlocked by the IRS for failing to (1) withhold the necessary amounts, and (2) regularly pay those funds to the proper government bodies. Yet there is a complete "Your Business Tax Kit," which is personally made up for you when you apply for your employer's identification tax number at your local IRS. The kit (which used to be called "Mr. Businessman's Tax Kit" but now has changed its name in recognition of women's changing business interests), contains all the tax forms and regulations that your particular type of business requires. Included is Circular E, "The Employer's Tax Guide," which contains the tables for social security and income withholding that Nancy had mentioned. Everything is free for the asking. "We're anxious to help you stay in business," a state IRS public relations man told me. "It spreads the tax load."

Soon after they moved to their office, the partners hired a creative artist to do the design, drawings, and layouts for the brochures, cover designs, package designs, annual reports, and other items they were trying to obtain orders for. Till then, their only employees had been hourly workers. When possible, hourly help is an excellent way for a new business to control cash outlay and overhead during the crucial formative months and perhaps even years. Nancy recalled, "Hiring that man as our creative person was a big step to us. Now we had someone on salary. That meant we needed business every day, no slow time."

I was puzzled. "You seem to have felt capable of doing everything else from bookkeeping to paste-up. How is it you didn't try to do the creative work?" I asked.

"We just knew we couldn't. We knew we needed help there."

Some 16 percent of business failure is caused by "unbalanced experience." No matter how strong you are in some aspects, you can fail completely if you are weak in others. For example, a retail owner may be an expert salesperson and know nothing about buying or proper markup or advertising. An entrepreneur may be able to counter weakness through study, training, and active seeking of information. However, if self-study is not practical or does not yield results fast enough, the businessperson who wants to succeed must obtain a partner or hire an assistant who is strong in those areas in which she or he is weak. Says Dr. Orlick, "Only in this way can they hope to offset the negative effects of unbalanced experience."

"After that we just kept growing," says Nancy. "Today we have fifteen people on salary. We've expanded to two floors. We do all kinds of work, from brochures, advertisements, annual reports, cover and package designs, hardbound books, and lots more. Last year we grossed a quarter of a million dollars."

"A quarter of a million dollars? But how did you build from a tiny beginning, where a four-thousand-dollar bank loan was an 'immense' amount of money, to two hundred and fifty thousand dollars gross annually?

"Partly by keeping old accounts through good service. Every printer we got when we first started out is still a customer. Then we built on that. They tell people. And when someone we worked with at any company left and went to a new job, we would contact them at the new place. They're already satisfied with our work. So, often new accounts are added through their recommendation to their new company. When things were slow, we tried mailings—not too successful for us. And we hustled. We went personally to see customers, told them we were slow, offered quick service and a little better price if they'd give us some work now. And we were constantly watching for special needs or services they might want that we could add and fill for them."

Nancy's husband had entered the living room and heard my exclamation about a quarter of a million annual gross. In a tone that suggested permanent surprise of his own, he added, "They've done it by themselves. They're as good as anybody in the business world. What's more important their bottom line is a lot stronger than many."

2
What You Need to Know
About Getting Started
and About Your
Business Personality

Unlike Nancy De Vries and Lynda Thomas, Bernice Evianda knew exactly what her goals were when she opened her business. "I wanted that specialty dress store to make me a lot of money." Bernice had worked as a dress salesgirl before she married. Later, she had operated a small dress business from her home basement for a few years until a town ordinance outlawed home retail efforts. And she had always been a passionate shopper.

"In fact, that's what gave me my idea. I never part with the straight retail price for any of my clothes. It would hurt my pride. I'll drive thirty miles to a shoe discount outlet for designer shoes. I've gone fifty miles for designer winter coats to a discount place that buys quality manufacturers' overcut or prestige stores' overstock. I know every quality store, factory, and loft discount outlet for fifty to sixty miles around here. I use the throughways. It's no problem.

"Yet my friends are like most people. They won't bother. They'll admire my bargains, but they won't bother to chase them. 'It's too far to drive,' they say. One day I said to myself, 'Why not open a quality discount women's clothing store in this town and make a fortune? The nearest competition is twenty-two miles away, and there are plenty of people with good incomes right here.' I haven't made the fortune yet. But I'm on my way. I've been in business three years." A plump, dark-haired woman, turned out in a high fashion jacket, skirt, and jewelry-accented outfit, Bernice is a splendid self-advertisement for her wares.

Getting Free Practical Guidance

Though she had bought stock for her home dress business, been a salesgirl for others, and spent years on her personal bargain hunts, Bernice took the precaution, before she acted, of collecting business advice from her nearest Small Business Administration office. "I pay taxes. Why shouldn't I get all the free advice and guides they hand out?" she says. Everything Bernice collected (and more) is available to everyone.

SBA No. 115A is a list of dozens of *free*, expertly written brochures; some examples include:

Building Repeat Retail Business
Building Strong Relations with Your Bank
Controlling Inventory in Small Wholesale Firms
Factors in Considering a Shopping Center Location
Preventing Retail Theft
Stock Control for Small Stores
Using a Traffic Study to Select a Retail Site

"Small Business Bibliographies," all free, each focus on a specific business. Bernice took:

Apparel and Accessories for Women, Misses & Children
Retail Credit and Collection.
Retailing

Someone else with another business in mind might have taken:

Handicrafts
Hobby Shops
Home Businesses
Motels
National Mailing-List Houses
Restaurants & Catering
Selling by Mail Order

SBA No. 115B gives lists of nominally priced, in-depth guides written by experts. These include an entire series of "Starting and

Managing," each directed at a different business. Bernice's "Starting and Managing a Small Business of Your Own" contained 97 pages of valuable facts for $1.35.

Other women could have chosen from the following, among many others:

Starting and Managing a Pet Shop, 40 pages, $.60
Starting and Managing a Small Bookkeeping Service, 64 pages, $.90
Starting and Managing a Small Retail Jewelry Store, 118 pages, $1.30.
Starting and Managing a Swap Shop or Consignment Sale Shop, 78 pages, $.95

To put herself on the permanent mailing list for future free management assistance publications, Bernice took half a minute to write her name and address (once) on the request form.

Avoiding Mistakes

To check some of her ideas and monetary estimates, Bernice asked for the free SBA counseling. Bernice's counselor might have been assigned from SBA's Service Corp of Retired Executives (SCORE) or Active Corp of Executives (ACE) groups, both of which offer their services without charge. The SCORE counselors are former owners and managers of businesses of every kind: retail, wholesale, service, and manufacturing. They are also men and women in engineering, accounting, law, science, finance, personnel, market research, advertising, public relations, and business management. "There is no phase of business in which we don't have some people with outstanding business records," Dr. Orlick had told me. ACE, the corp of currently active practitioners in all the above categories, supplements SCORE's services with knowledge of the newest machines and practices in each occupation.

Bernice's counselor was a SCORE man with more than 40 years of experience in the women's wear business, 25 of them as owner-manager of a successful store. Together they looked over

Bernice's answers to the 23-page "Business Plan for Retailers," an SBA workbook-type brochure which you, the prospective businessperson, are invited to judge your readiness by filling in the answers to your business plan for such categories as these: Determining the Sales Potential, Attracting Customers, In-Store Sales Promotion, Your Plan for Buying (for example, will a manufacturer sell you three coats for stock, or are you going to be stunned to discover you must accept a dozen? Better find out now), Behind-the-Scenes Work, Estimated Cash Forecast (a retail business in contrast to a service enterprise requires considerable cash invested in inventory), Break-Even Point, Is Your Plan Workable? °

The counselor had a C.P.A. colleague suggest a simplified bookkeeping system that Bernice was unfamiliar with, and he suggested an ACE counselor to help her with advertising, a business aspect she had no experience with.

Her original counselor also made a suggestion that Bernice now believes may have been the difference between her current success and possible failure. "Because I thought nothing of driving miles and miles for a bargain, I didn't properly understand about locating my store. I had picked a very low-rent place down a quiet side street two full blocks from the main shopping area. I figured, 'What's two blocks when I have all those great bargains?'

"The SCORE counselor convinced me I was better off paying rent in the main traffic area even if it meant adding a dollar or two to my prices. He said that's one of the commonest retail mistakes. He had me laughing. He asked me, 'Why not rent a spot in the Sahara for a dollar a year? Maybe only one customer on only one camel a year will go by, but you'll have a fantastic rent bargain.' He also said that choosing your store location because it's convenient for you or close to your home is another very common mistake. The people it's got to be convenient for are the customers."

Since one of the SBA sponsored Management Seminars for Small Business was beginning at a nearby college, he also suggested that Bernice attend the five lectures: Starting and

---

° There are three other business plan workbook brochures; for small service firms, for small manufacturers, and for small construction firms. SBA's definition of "small business" extends from one-person operations on up to include 95 percent of American businesses.

Managing a Small Business of Your Own, Managing Your Finances, Advertising and Promoting Your Business, Legal Problems in Small Business, and Marketing in Today's Small Business Economy. Each SBA office (see the complete address list in appendix) sponsors dozens, sometimes hundreds, of varied seminars in its territory each year. If she had wanted or needed it, Bernice Evianda could have obtained guidance from her SBA counselors for a year or several years, without charge. She could also have applied for an SBA business loan. However, the SBA encourages you to use its loan program only as a last resort if your own savings, friends, relatives, and banks have all been unavailable or inadequate.

Do You Have the Successful Entrepreneur's Personality?

Bernice's open admission that she had created her business "to make a fortune" was a valuable attitude for an entrepreneur. A belief that money is very important has been found to be a necessity for successful business ownership. Without this belief, owners lack the psychological stamina to drive themselves when they must work long hours, attend to tedious details, live with tough decisions, and when treadmill stick-to-it means the difference between failure and success.

In the last chapter we discussed Dr. Witkins's observation that entrepreneurial and executive women excel at business independence and cool-headed decision making. Other studies have pinpointed other personality characteristics and attitudes that all successful entrepreneurs of both sexes must possess.

Bernice Evianda had a chance to self-check some of these traits when she answered the 10 personality questions contained in the SBA "Checklist for Going into Business" leaflet, Small Marketer's Aid No. 71.

Choose one answer for each question:

Are you a self starter?
1. I do things on my own. Nobody has to tell me to get going.
2. If someone gets me started, I keep going all right.

3. Easy does it, man. I don't put myself out until I have to.

How do you feel about other people?
 1. I like people. I can get along with just about anybody.
 2. I have plenty of friends—I don't need anyone else.
 3. Most people bug me.

Can you take responsibility?
 1. I like to take charge of things and see them through.
 2. I'll take over if I have to, but I'd rather let someone else be responsible.
 3. There's always some eager beaver around wanting to show how smart he is. I say let him.

How good an organizer are you?
 1. I like to have a plan before I start. I'm usually the one to get things lined up when the gang wants to do something.
 2. I do all right unless things get too goofed up. Then I cop out.
 3. You get all set, and then something comes along and blows the whole bag. So I just take things as they come.

How good a worker are you?

 1. I can keep going as long as I need to. I don't mind working hard for something I want.
 2. I'll work hard for a while, but when I've had enough, that's it man.
 3. I can't see that hard work gets you anywhere.

The other five questions are the following: Can you make decisions? Can you stick with it? Can people trust what you say? How good is your health? Can you lead others?

The interpretation of your answers reads like this:

If most of your checks are beside the first answers, you probably have what it takes to run a business. If not, you're likely to have more trouble than you can handle by yourself.

Better find a partner who is strong on the points you're weak on. If many checks are beside the third answer, not even a good partner will be able to shore you up.

Then there is the question of whether psychologically you have the temperament to live comfortably with all the uncertainties of business ownership. Psychological experiments indicate that your own self-appraisal can be very helpful. Researchers have discovered that people who must have the security of a job and a regular paycheck and consequently cannot cope emotionally with business ownership have temperaments that *they themselves* describe as cooperative, determined, deliberate, efficient, self-controlled, poised, and stable. People who can take business chances and uncertainties in their stride and who do not require the cushion of job security tend to see themselves as being important, courageous, sharp-witted, clear-thinking, imaginative, ingenious, and foresighted. Which type of person are you?

Life Experience

None of the studies have a category for "life experience," but Bernice Evianda, Nancy De Vries, and Dr. Orlick all had similar reactions when I asked them, "Is there a difference between a man or woman entrepreneur?" "Not intrinsically," said Dr. Orlick. "The only difference may be in what life experiences she has had. The woman who has had little experience outside her home may have every other personality trait necessary, but until she gets some worldly business seasoning, she is at a serious disadvantage."

Nancy put it this way: "Every volunteer activity experience a woman has is an asset in going into business. Everything she's been involved in outside her home gives her experience in relating to people other than on the mother/housewife wave-length. Volunteer work has another strength. You have a chance at all kinds of organizational responsibilities and executive work. It's less expensive and painful to make mistakes and learn in that world than in business."

Said Bernice, "When you've had experience in the business

world and understand the way people behave there and understand office politics and business competition, then you're ready to go into business for yourself. Everything that you ever did in your life up to this date dealing with people, with problems, with money, is experience that gives you a head start."

3
Strategies for Coping

Coping with Your Business

Your business success story, like every business success story, will have its individual twists. Mildred Mulcock, who built a small-town bridal-gown salon into one of the United State's largest independent bridal enterprises, which draws customers from three states and has annual sales of $400,000, says that, in a business like hers, "advertising, promotion, fashion shows, knowledgeable buying—this is where you have to come across to beat the competition." You must also be litmus-sensitive to your customers' needs. After the recent recession, the $300 gowns, which had been Mildred's most popular price range, yielded to the $175 to $200 gowns. If she hadn't noticed and adjusted her buying accordingly, she could have had a disastrous year.

Successful free-lance self-employment would represent the "impossible dream" come true for many women. Whether it's a creative business career in art, photography, writing, or a craft, or a practical career as a free-lance travel agent, bookkeeper, businessperson, and so on, self-discipline makes the crucial difference.

As the famous remark puts it, "A man sitting in his study is working and cannot be disturbed; a woman sitting in her study is a mother who is available." The exact way you get control of your time is up to you, but unless you do it, you cannot succeed as a home-based free lance. Many women free lancers who succeed teach themselves to go to their work the minute the last child leaves for school in the morning. One successful writer told me, "It used to kill me to leave the breakfast dishes there, the house unpicked up, but I finally found it's the only way. When the children walk in at three, I can pay attention to them and talk to them while I'm moving around the house straightening, doing the laundry, and making dinner." Then she added, "Teaching your friends and relatives not to phone during your working hours can be an uphill battle but you've got to win it."

A free-lance public relations woman explains how she finds assignments. "I worked in a public relations firm before my second child was born. Now I get jobs from former contacts. I also find jobs from following newspaper ads. When I see an ad asking for a public relations director, I call the firm, even though I don't want the job, and try to make an appointment to discuss an assignment. I figure if they're looking for a director, things must be less than perfect in the office, and they may need outside help.

"Another good way I've found is to call public relations agencies when I'm working on an assignment for someone else. I'll call and ask if they have a client who would be appropriate to be quoted as an expert in my current assignment. It doesn't matter whether they do or don't. I've now self-introduced myself to them as a working public relations person. I have a chance to chat, make an appointment to go up and meet with them, and see what assignments they might be able to give me.

A New Mexico commercial artist explained to me during a phone interview, "As a free lance in business on your own, besides self-discipline, you can't be timid. In fact, you need a certain amount of push, either natural or acquired in order to keep yourself in work."

Del Goetz is a divorced former model, sports-car racer, and bank research director who bought a failing moving and used furniture company. For her, business turnaround depended on 18 months of Scrooge-like cost cutting and tight management. She cut labor costs by 50 percent by using an hourly pay system instead of salary and by washing windows, unloading trucks, and even cleaning the bathrooms herself.

Other women see their "impossible dream" not primarily as a moneymaker but as a part-time occupation that will provide a passageway to the lifestyle they yearn for. Says Wilma Collins of her home-based Florida art gallery, "With me, it's not primarily the money. It's useful certainly. But all my life I've dreamt of running an art gallery. I love the artists and other people I meet, the daily routine, the social life it gives me access to." From the practical viewpoint, Wilma explains that her volunteer contacts have been the difference between success and failure. "I soon found I couldn't create a going business out of an art gallery in my ten-by-thirteen family room. I didn't want to undertake the full-time pressures of renting a store and making it pay. Instead, through my volunteer contacts, I now arrange art shows and art auctions as fund-raisers for the volunteer organizations. I'm doing one now for the town Cancer Drive. I get all my art on consignment from the artist; until I sell it, it costs me nothing. When I arrange the shows for the charity, the artist is guaranteed a certain price, I get my commission, and the charity gets its share. Now that I'm established, I can approach volunteer groups I've had no previous personal contact with."

A Different View: Coping with Home and Family

There are probably as many methods for coping with home, family, and career as there are women. As we mentioned in Section I, entire books have been written on the subject. The gist of these books, from the lighthearted to the scholarly, is that with rare, enlightened exceptions, even in families where a husband enthusiastically supports a wife's career and physically helps, he sees himself as doing just that: "helping.' It is she who is "in charge" or "responsible for" home and children. Its myriad details are on her mind, not his.

In her book *Working Mothers* (New York: Doubleday, 1976), Jean Curtis interviewed 200 families with working mothers and has loosely classified husbands into four groups. As she sees them, Group A are the "professionals." They have taken their role as husband to a working wife seriously. They spout feminist philosophy, accept all the principles of an egalitarian marriage, and work hard at becoming a psychologically aware parent. They work so grimly at it that, she says, they also have a high divorce rate. Husbands in Group B know little about feminist jargon or issues. They believe women "ought to be treated well," but they do not brood about it. They pull most of their weight in a household, but chores are usually traditionally divided. In Group C are "supportive" husbands, in the sense that they cheer their wives' accomplishments and think it's "okay" for their wives to work as long as they "can keep up with everything else—the kids, the cooking, the house, and some sort of social life." Group D husbands are "otherwise known as 'the boys'. . . . Any working mother married to one of 'the boys' has got an impossibly demanding life. . . . He can barely smother his anxiety and embarrassment at having a working wife. They never do anything unless the chore is 'manful' like painting the *outside* of the house or fixing an appliance."

Jean Curtis has reported *what* is happening in American homes with working wives and mothers. Another researcher, sociologist Catherine Arnott, has approached husbands' behavior from another angle: Why? In a study published in the highly respected research publication *Journal of Marriage and the Family* ("Husbands' Attitude and Wives' Commitment to Employment," November, 1972), she set out to test the hypothesis that "married women seek to make their role preference congruent with that of their husband. The study also examined the effect of wives' attitude to autonomy for women on their expectations as to which partner should adjust when there is tension or conflict over her role."

Through a "purposive selection" of women's clubs, a broad range of women were surveyed in terms of commitment to employment and attitude to autonomy for women. Mail-back questionnaires were given the women, together with questionnaires for their husbands. Dr. Arnott received 235 completed questionnaires, most of which included the husbands' also. After studying and charting the questionnaires, she discovered the following (which the scholarly journal reported in typically academic language): "The hypothesis that shared husband-wife role preference leads to role continuity or change, depending on whether this preference was for her present role or a different one, was strongly supported."

In English, that sentence, together with some accompanying flourishes in other sentences, means this: The way your husband reacts to your working may depend on how strongly you yourself believe in the equality of men and women.

The mini-test below, which Dr. Arnott used as part of her study, can give you some insight into your own self-view. If you were working, which solutions to home and career conflicts would you arrive at?

Choose *as many* as seem appropriate:

1. Trying to make it up to your husband.
2. Doing better on 'all fronts.'
3. Trying to separate home and work.
4. Expect your husband to accept less perfection at home.
5. Expect him to help you more.
6. Expect him to see your problem of carrying both home and outside responsibilities.

Women who believe strongly in equality usually choose 4, 5, and 6, which require the husband to help in the family adjustment to the wife's home-and-career life. Choosing 1, 2, and 3, which depend entirely on the wife's efforts, suggests that you are unsure of your right to a wifely role that is nontraditional and that you are inevitably conveying this attitude to your husband, whose behavior then, in part at least, reflects your attitude.

"Yet," writes Dr. Arnott, "the wives in the study who were pressing toward a more liberal marriage were as interested as traditional wives in living up to their husbands' expectations. They might believe in self-determination but they did not seem inclined to flaunt their feelings. *Their success in developing a cooperative attitude from their husbands seemed to be the result of the wives' willingness to talk conflicts out rather than trying to work around the problems. In short, they often lived up to their husbands' expectations by changing the men's standards* [emphasis added]. The liberal wives' belief that their husbands should be willing to contribute to the family adjustment seems to make the couple skillful at hammering out innovative relationships. And the husbands often respond with pride in their wives' accomplishments and individuality."

A major surprise, according to Dr. Arnott, was the discovery that while conservative wives pleased their husbands by living according to the women's-place-is-in-the-home rules, the liberal women seemed to succeed better than the moderate women. Though 60 percent of the liberal women reported that their lifestyles led to a "meaningful relationship" with their husbands (71 percent for the conservatives), only 44 percent of the moderates felt that way about the results of their own lifestyles.

"It is the moderate women," reports Dr. Arnott, "the women in the middle who try to straddle the old and the new wife roles without really being committed to either, who seem to have the most trouble pleasing themselves and their husbands. They are the ones who seem to be bearing the brunt of rapid social change in the lifestyles of women."

The moral seems to be this: For your own and for your husband's happiness, too, get off the fence and pick a point of view.

Coping with Co-Workers and Business Contacts

Industrial psychologists refer to a common phenomenon that they call the "halo effect." The halo effect causes people, both men and women, to believe that "if that person has that job, he/ she must be suited to its prestige and demands." Though both men and women are subject to the "halo's" immediate influence, men rapidly learn to check the person's suitability for the position and make their own independent judgment. Women whose lives have centered in their homes usually have no comparable experience. As Nancy De Vries expressed it near the end of our three-hour interview, "At the beginning I was somewhat intimidated by people that I was seeing, that I was trying to sell a service to, because in my mind they had a kind of ivory-tower position. They were in a regular job, and I was a housewife starting out.

"I often felt disappointed. Most of the people we do business with are men, probably ninety percent of them. And when we were starting, I was intimidated by their positions, by their companies, by the whole thing. It's as if this thing is up there, and you come up and you stand there in awe of it. I don't know how aware of it I was at that time. Looking back on it now, I see that I was awed.

"And because everything seemed so important and I was intimidated by it, I was often disappointed. I expected that these people worked in ivory towers. Many times I was confused while working with these businessmen. The ivory tower disappeared and I was left disappointed yet still impressed by their positions. In other words, I was putting a kind of mental label on them which left me in a subservient role. I now know the difference.

"I now know another thing, too. Now I can tell people I will or will not meet their business conditions. That I can't make delivery at that date, or that their project budget is too tight and I need more money to do the job. I can come back at them on the same level and expect them to answer me with respect. In the beginning I didn't have that position. Or I thought I didn't. I often felt unsure of myself. I've learned, too, that I can make business specifications and guidelines that I can expect other people to adhere to, that I don't just have to accept or reject the guidelines they give me.

"Particularly for me as a woman, one of the things that hit me the most was the elevated status I mentally gave to businessmen or what I then viewed as an elevated position. When I actually worked on a project, I found my evaluations changing and that I was certainly their equal.

"Now that I understand this factor, I am better able to listen, to learn from my peers in the business world. I find I am more open, more confident, and more businesslike. It was so conflicting. So confusing. I had trouble with that in the beginning. I really did.

"And I think a lot of women start out with that attitude. You're home and these men are going off to work. You don't really understand the facts because you haven't been out there. You have this kind of feeling that they're going to work and that this is big stuff and all that kind of nonsense. You go out there and you meet them, and it's just not all that big. I don't like to say that. But that's what I was faced with—that kind of distortion. What I had viewed as 'a man's job' and what I was discovering out there didn't match. It wasn't so spectacular or so deserving of the respect I was treating the business world with."

I asked, "Was it the job that wasn't as important as you thought or the person wasn't as competent as he should have been?"

"Both," she said. "I was allowing them more respect and awe than was really necessary or warranted. I've learned over the years that I'm as good as they are, and sometimes better. I'm as talented, as deserving of respect, and I get it."

APPENDIX:

THE ETIQUETTE OF OFFICE POLITICS AND OTHER USEFUL INFORMATION

1
The Etiquette of
Office Politics

It is not just that women lack confidence in their work skills. They are cautious about attempting to get really good jobs because they know instinctively that the rules in the work world are different from those in personal, social life. But they do not know what the business rules are. Since these new rules are largely based on unspoken assumptions, the first weeks and months can be perplexing for a woman making the transition from home social behavior to business behavior unless she is armed with the essential facts.

Following are the necessary basic facts that should make for an easy transition from managing a home to juggling a home plus job. In the pages titled "Succeeding Once You Have Your Middle or Top Job" later in this section, you will find a list of some books on the subject that you may also find useful.

An Office Is Not a Home

The main thing to remember is that an office is not a home. (Everything that is discussed here and hereafter about an office applies with equal force to a store, school, hospital, or any work setting you might be in. Only the details of locale and job assignment will vary. Human behavior and motives remain the same.) People are in an office to make money, to protect their jobs, and, if possible, to use their present job as a stepping stone to a better job. Though they are not out to get you personally, if you and your goals stand between them and their goals, you have to recognize it and then keep your wits about you. The person who forgets this cannot accurately react to or understand those around her.

If you are in a noncompetitive work pool, where many of you are doing the same kind of work with little or no chance for advancement, then, yes, it is very possible that you can make good personal friends. Or, if you meet someone in another department of your company who in no way competes with or deals with your area, then, yes, again, it is possible that you two may become personal friends.

But as soon as you and the possible friend are working in situations where you both are competing for an order, for a promotion, for your personal production record as against that person's production record, then you can relax and have lunch together and talk fashions and husbands and children, but a part of you has to be aware that *on a business level* you are rivals, not friends.

At the same time, always keep in mind that it is your responsibility to get along pleasantly with the people you work with. In my years of writing on job psychology and interviewing numerous business employment experts, I have heard the same analysis many times: "More people lose their jobs and fail to get promotions because of personality clashes than because of incompetence." Or to put it positively, "Acceptance is often more important than competence."

It does not make any difference to your boss if you are "right" or "wrong." Once you become a center of dissension, you lose your value to a supervisor. You are interfering with production and office morale. When other people battle with each other, your best course is neutrality. In his book *How to Get Along with (Almost) Everybody* (New York: American Management Associations, 1973) Elton Reeves points out that in winning acceptance of co-workers many people make the mistake of believing they can look their fellow workers over once, come to their private decisions, and then expect the situations "to be set in concrete ever after." Reeves suggests that these are fluid situations that you must be constantly aware of. He offers some rules to help: (1)Be intellectually honest. This means being careful not to deliberately 'misunderstand' and avoiding gossip in which you delicately twist interpretations of what others did or said. (2) Be sure you pass on all necessary information. This, says Reeves, can do more to tear down or build up your reputation with others than anything else. (3) Be positive. People usually react on the same emotional level you use in approaching them. (4) Don't expect too much in the way of active friendship. In general, this is a work relationship, and all that is necessary is that you go through the day together amiably. "You will be most successful if you take the attitude that the greatest responsibility for your acceptance or rejection by others rests on your shoulders."

Should You Confide in Your Co-Workers?

Whether or not you confide in your co-workers depends on the particular situation. There are some things you might want to tell your co-workers and your supervisor, and other things you would be wise to keep to yourself even if you almost choke on them. Trying to develop a special relationship with your boss by acting as a personal listening post usually backfires. Telling supervisors "what people are saying" about them will definitely earn you a special spot, as a gossip and troublemaker. However, if a jealous co-worker circulates tales about you that are *serious,* you might quietly confide in your boss. No histrionics, just calm passing on of information. (But, again, what you are really aiming for is zero personality clashes.) Bosses may do nothing about situations like this when they learn of them; yet their knowledge will protect you when the false rumbles reach their ears.

Personal troubles are a whole category of their own. If there is serious illness in your family, it may be right to let people know. You may think you are behaving normally at work despite your worries, but others may notice erratic actions. If they understand the cause, they will be more willing to overlook *occasional* lapses. They will not, however, expect you to behave "like a worried mother" all day. If you are being paid to work and produce, that is what they will expect you to be doing.

When you are beset by marital and romantic difficulties or embarrassing legal, monetary, or personal dilemmas, do not be too quick to let it all pour out. The one person you are telling it to may be all right. But what about that one person's other good friend, who will soon be hearing the story? And the next person? Why compound your difficulties by soiling your image at work? Then you will have two problems instead of one.

The Power Chart

Every business company, every office, has two power charts: the official one and the real one. One of the bits of nonsense that is constantly served up about the United States concerns our having no class system. Whereas the Old World feudal class system is built into military and social lives, ours is soldered into our business life. It affects who talks to whom during coffee breaks and where, who lunches together, and even who walks down the hall together. Most important, it affects where the real power lies.

The official power chart of any business group is published for all to peruse. However, only quiet, persistent observation of how decisions are made and who controls the discussion and information will eventually bring you to an understanding of the real power structure. Often a secretary to a key official or someone with a mediocre-sounding title actually wields immense power.

It is necessary for you, the newcomer, to shed your private ideas about social hierarchy, which are totally irrelevant here. Quietly look around and learn where you and everybody else stand in that particular organization. Every group functions differently. Just watch and then do as the others do. One of the wisest pieces of business advice insists that you be pleasant to everybody not only because you are a civilized, nice human being, but also because little Miss Nobody today may be the assistant in a key department of your best customer tomorrow; and the office boy may some day be the clerk in the boss's office, through whom your plans and requests must pass.

Cooperation

Does all this mean that your days are a constant scenario of skirmishes? No, as a matter of fact, in order to flourish you have to learn to cooperate and share your knowledge discreetly. Otherwise others may come to see you as a cold and even hostile person and respond to you accordingly. Though the business world is certainly not a land of undiluted kindness, you do have to be flexible in judging co-workers' motives. Many people who will want to talk to you about business ideas are simply attempting to share the excitement of the day's activities. And constantly being too shrewd to allow anyone "to pick your brains" when people come to you with business questions means that when *you* need business answers, you are left wondering, "Why won't anyone cooperate?"

Your ideas about "character" can also unintentionally separate you from others. If you believe that asking for or accepting help at work marks a person as weak or incompetent, your contempt for people who accept aid will show. Because your attitude is "I'm strong, so I'll do it myself," you may even lock yourself into isolation.

Your behavior during inevitable job crises is also important. Withholding facts and help that might bring the other person safely through may make your own performance look fine by contrast. But word gets around. There will come a day when *you* need emergency back-up and cooperation.

People Have All Kinds of Motives

When you start your new job, you may find that everyone is genuinely pleased to have you aboard. It certainly happens that way very often, as it did to Adele Lerner, Gloria Brager, Eloise Garrity, Marian Burden, Emily Menninger, Karen Ostrow and to many other women we have discussed. But if you discover that you have some ready-made enemies, people who dislike you the minute you show up, do not take it personally. There are many reasons for business tensions that have nothing whatsoever to do with you. First, be on guard for the secret enemy who appears to be your friend and, during the first buddy-buddy lunches, tells you all the office rules that "nobody bothers to observe." You may hear that "no one ever comes to department meetings on time," and then you stroll in to your first meeting five minutes late to find everyone assembled, waiting tensely for you! Your "friend" has seen to it that you will never be a rival.

Causes of enmity that have nothing to do with you as an individual can include the following: (1) Jealousy. Your co-worker would shoot at anyone holding your job. Though not qualified for the position you hold, your opponent would like to have it. (2) Revenge. This kind of person is qualified for your job, but was unable to obtain it. By discrediting you, your co-worker hopes to push you out and make another try for it. (3) Pride. Someone who had a say voted against your getting the job. Now, because of hurt pride, that person is determined to see you fail to vindicate his or her original judgment against you. (4) "That's not the way I did it!" Your work style is different from that of someone who once held your job or a job similar to yours. Therefore, you must be "wrong." 5) "You're not going to show me up!" You are obviously competent.

How to Look Good at a Meeting

Always be "for" something, never against. If you feel you must try to eliminate a poor idea, do not attack it. Instead, *support* another approach. This is necessary because no matter how logical an attack may be, it leaves you with a negative and obstructionist image. Every time you speak at a meeting, remember the other people there probably feel as vulnerable as you do. They will resent even the slightest criticism. If you want to offer a better idea, save the previous speakers' egos by building your idea on theirs: "What's been said is very good, and could we also consider. . . ."

How to Dress

The woman who knows she is competent and should be considered for promotion and increased responsibility has to dress the part. Many women who have mastered the skills of their jobs have not yet matched their wardrobes to their career expectations. If a woman hopes to be taken seriously at her job, she has to realize that her clothes help *create* other people's opinion of her. Super-casual clothes, seductive clothes, drab and mousy clothes, kooky clothes—all fail to suggest job ability. The key word is "appropriate." What is right at an advertising agency might be wrong at a staid insurance firm. A woman must also understand that nothing is more obsolete than the idea of a career woman as a severe-looking, unattractive female. In today's business world, good-looking clothes and the right makeup and hairstyling are valuable. By choosing an appearance that projects an attractive, competent aura, a woman helps her co-workers and her bosses see her as the capable person she is.

2
Where the Jobs Will Be: Now to 1985

When you invent a job, as the women in this book did, you find that no occupation is overcrowded. As we saw, though standard teaching positions are in extremely short supply, Karen Ostrow, by creating the job of teaching drama to children, rapidly found not one employer but four.

However, if you want to study the possibilities for standard job opportunities, the United States government's *Occupational Outlook Handbook*, available in many libraries or from any Bureau of Labor Statistics regional office can help you concentrate on the best possibilities. The handbook carefully reports the job prospects for 850 different occupations, as labor experts see them, from now through 1985. Before you invest time, energy, and tuition payments preparing, find out what the outlook is for various careers. The women who struggled through to teaching degrees during the last few years could have saved themselves disappointment by glancing at this book. As long ago as 1970, the teaching glut was forecast. What does the future hold for the job or career that you have in mind?

For a copy of the *Occupational Outlook Handbook*, make your check or money order ($7.00) payable to Superintendent of Documents, and send it either to Suite 3400, 1515 Broadway, New York, New York 10036; or to Federal Building, 911 Walnut Street, 16th floor, Kansas City, Missouri 64106. Other regional offices are located in Boston, Atlanta, Philadelphia, Chicago, Dallas, and San Francisco. If you are in any of these areas, you may visit the office and consult the handbook there.

3
Analyzing Your
Job Aptitudes
and Job Temperament

It is a mistake to believe that you can do anything you set your mind to. You have certain natural aptitudes and your own personality. You should choose an occupation in which they will be an asset. If you follow the wrong signs, you can easily end up in an occupation where you will constantly have to suppress your natural talents, constantly have to work against your natural inclinations.

For example, if you have a strong imagination and creative ability, you should avoid occupations that demand a steady level of straightforward concentration and in which a strong imagination has been found to be a *handicap*. Your mind will "wander," causing you to make mistakes that affect your performance record. Emotionally you will find the endless, unvarying routine is a burden that causes you to tolerate rather than enjoy your work. Positions for highly imaginative people to *avoid* include accountant, bookkeeper, computer programmer, business executive, administrator, physician, manager, supervisor, typist, auditor, banker, lawyer. Far more compatible with their temperaments are selling, teaching, writing, design, interviewing, and any occupation that provides an opportunity to talk with people and think up new ideas, techniques, products, or methods.

These facts, and many more, have been discovered by the nonprofit organization mentioned earlier, the Johnson O'Connor Research Foundation, during their half century of job aptitude testing and follow-up of half a million people. A complete individual analysis is expensive, but you may find it a wise investment. For approximately $200 you receive three days of testing and individual counseling, which provides you with a thorough insight into your own abilities.

A friend of mine had her 18-year-old daughter tested. She said, "Suddenly, for the first time we could comprehend the mixture of aptitude strengths and weaknesses that had previously baffled us. She was planning to study business administration in college, with a major in international business. For this, she expected to learn Russian and some Chinese. We discovered that her natural aptitude for learning languages is very low. But her high imagination and other aptitudes make her a natural for a business marketing major. It saved her years of floundering, and so was money well invested." The same might well be true for you; such an analysis could put you immediately on the right course as you start "in the middle." Since the lifespan for the average woman now reaches deep into the seventies, even women in their forties and fifties have decades of life ahead of them. Many women in their forties still have as many years ahead of them as they have already lived.

Centers for the Johnson O'Connor Research Foundation, (sometimes listed as "Human Engineering Laboratories") are located in the following cities: Boston, Philadelphia, New York, Washington, D.C., Atlanta, Chicago, Detroit, Ft. Worth, Houston, Tulsa, Los Angeles, and San Diego. Their publications are mailed from the Boston office (Human Engineering Laboratory, 347 Beacon Street, Boston, Massachusetts 02167).

For a shortcut to many of the Johnson O'Connor facts that you can then apply to yourself, pick up the book *Be Yourself: Analyze Your Innate Aptitudes* by Margaret Broadley (Washington, D.C., and New York: Robert B. Luce, Inc., 1972, $5.95; in case you wish to send for it, the address is 750 Third Avenue, New York, New York 10017). Written in a chatty, fun style, it describes what the human engineering researchers have learned about the type of personality and aptitudes you need to be happy as a lawyer, businessperson, artist, secretary, salesperson, and so on. This is a don't-miss book.

A different kind of publication, a workbook titled *How to Decide: A Guide for Women* by Nelle Tumlin Scholz, Judith Sosebee Prince, and Gordon Porter Miller, is published by the

College Entrance Examination Board (888 Seventh Avenue, New York, New York 10019, softcover, $5.95). Through filling in answers to questions, you learn decision-making techniques, find out what you want, develop a plan of action, recognize how to cope with value conflicts, and discover your interests, abilities, and special talents.

Other Ideas for Assessing Your Skills

If you find you are still having trouble focusing on exactly what you do best, *Get the Best of Yourself* by Katherine Nash (New York: Grosset & Dunlap, 1976, $8.95) shows you how to think back over your school experiences, work life, friendships, and community and home life to those experiences that have given you deep satisfaction. The book then helps you discover what aspects of those experiences you most enjoyed. Finally, you develop your "success pattern" for what you do best, which in turn leads to job ideas.

With minor variations, this basic approach of discovering your success pattern and then building a job campaign and resume upon what you discover is used by most women's job counseling organizations throughout the United States. Some of these organizations are volunteer or nonprofit, or both. Some are commercial groups. None actually provide jobs or job leads. None are employment agencies. They offer group guidance and companionship as you grope your way to self-knowledge and a job campaign.

For information about groups in your area, consult the following:

1. The adult education department of your local community college.
2. Better yet, the women's center, if one exists, at your community college. Chances are, the women's center itself offers such a service.
3. Your local Y.
4. The free booklet *Women's Centers: Where Are They?* (Association of American Colleges, 1818 R Street N.W.,

Washington, D.C. 20009), which helps locate the public service, nonprofit women's centers in your state and local area. Since women's centers are mushrooming, no publication provides the absolutely final list. This is the most complete list available.

California lists some 70 centers, New York 59, Illinois 34, Colorado 21, Kansas and Iowa 8 each, Maine 9, Connecticut 13, Alabama and Alaska 2 each, Wyoming and North Dakota 1 each. Of the 50 states, only South Dakota lacks a center, and that may have been remedied since the publication went to press.

5. Catalyst, a national organization dedicated to helping college-educated women combine career and home responsibilities. It publishes two useful 50- to 60-page softcover books: *Planning for Work,* Self-Guidance Series G1, which, again, through a workbook format and some good exposition, guides you through "self-exploration, self-assessment, readiness for action;" and *Your Job Campaign,* Self-Guidance Series G2, which deals with "getting started; overview of career fields, resume, interview, part-time possibilities, etc." ($1.25 each; 14 East 60th Street, New York, New York 10022).

Catalyst also publishes a series of individual pamphlets in the Career Opportunity Series, each of which covers training, opportunities, and other information in a specific occupation such as accounting, advertising, banking, and personnel ($1.25 each at above address).

Catalyst works with 157 resource centers for women located throughout the United States. All of the centers are autonomous.They provide education and career counseling, job referral, placement services. Some are free; some charge a fee. A complete list of the centers is available from Catalyst headquarters at the above address.

4
Finding the Job

First, before you tie up your time and mind with courses and programs and self-discovery charts, remember life does *not* have to be complicated. The best way, the simplest way, is the way followed by the hundreds of women discussed in this book. They recognized what they could do. They picked up the phone, called the person who could give them an opportunity, made an appointment, explained what they had to offer, and, presto, were hired. *You absolutely cannot beat this direct method for swiftness, simplicity, and superb results for getting the job you are best equipped for and will enjoy the most.*

As soon as you start working with the standard job-seeking tools, you lay yourself open to being judged by the standard criteria instead of by the criteria of your unique life experience, which the above method exploits. Nevertheless, if you would like to give yourself an overview of the conventional wisdoms and methods, some of the best follow:

1. *The Brain Watchers*, by Martin Gross (Random House, 201 E. 50 St. New York, New York 10022, $7.95). If you find yourself in line for an executive position, for which you may be subjected to one or more of the personality assessment psychological tests, help yourself beat the test with this book. Highly readable, this is the definitive popular treatment of the subject. The testers are looking for certain personality traits for certain positions. Rightly or wrongly, they have decided that to succeed, say, as a salesperson you must be optimistic, outgoing, not worrisome, not moody, but rather buoyantly extroverted, dominant, and high in

self-confidence. Gross, who made a three-year study of the tests and how they are scored, reports in his book that you must present yourself as near perfect as possible in the traits the job requires. For executive jobs, you can be sure employers are looking for your desire for "achievement." If you work more for the pay and what it will buy rather than out of a sense of pure "achievement," do not admit it. The tests throw curves at you like the following tough "achievement" choices: "Pick one: (A) I like to help my friends when they are in trouble. (B) I like to do my very best in whatever I undertake." Choose the "achiever" answer, B. This book, which is fun to read, tells you what the testers are looking for in most jobs. Then you can go in and give them what they want.

2. *Moving Up*, by Eli Djeddah (Philadelphia: J. B. Lippincott Company, 1971, $5.95). We quoted some of the ideas from this book in our "No Skills" section. Djeddah gives good techniques for finding the jobs you never hear about and for helping someone invent a job especially for you.

3. *The Hidden Job Market*, by Tom Jackson and Davidyne Mayleas (New York: Quadrangle, 1976). It describes just what the title indicates and provides a career Baedeker, besides. The book tells how to find the market and how to make use of it.

4. *If Not College, What? The Guide to Career Education* by Muriel Lederer (New York: Quadrangle, 1975, $10.95, paperback). This book lists 200 occupations, such as aeronautics, engineering, science technology, graphic communications, health services, business, agriculture, conservation, and many more; tells where you can fill technical, creative, and productive jobs *without a college degree;* describes each job, the technical education or training you need for it, and what it has to offer. *The book also contains a useful section on how to appraise a trade school, find the reliable ones, avoid the gyps.*

5. *Work When You Want to Work: The Complete Guide for the "Temporary" Worker* by John Fanning with George Sullivan, available from Uniforce, 41 East 42nd Street, New York, New York 10017, $1.25. The book explains everything you need to know about getting, holding, and making the most of job opportunities offered through the temporary job agencies.

Work When You Want To, Operational Services, Western

Temporary Services, Inc., P.O. Box 7737, San Francisco, California 94120; free, but enclose a stamped, self-addressed long envelope. An informative, easy-to-read brochure, this explains temporary work—what kinds of skills are needed, how to choose a temporary help service to work for, what you should know about skill tests, and how to brush up on your skills if necessary. The booklet also describes how to use temporary-help assignments as a way of finding a permanent job you will like, and how to work and travel simultaneously.

Self-Analyzer, Staff Builders, Inc., 122 East 42nd Street, New York, New York 10017. This is a three-page self-analyzing test that helps you discover which temporary business jobs you are best suited for and would enjoy most. You can get it free at any Staff Builders temporary personnel office, or write for a copy at the above address.

6. *How to Beat the Employment Game: Secrets of the Personnel Recruiters,* by David Noer (Radnor, Pa.: Chilton Book Company, 1975, $7.95). Recruiters, otherwise known as "headhunters," are the reverse of employment agencies. They are companies and individuals hired by corporations to locate executive talent. Because of affirmative action pressure, many businesses have the recruiters out searching for "qualified" women. In this book are the behind-the-scenes facts about interview games recruiters play and ways to handle tests, interviews, and reference checks. In a breezy style, the author, an experienced "headhunter" himself, tells you the motives and strategies of the recruiters and how to turn events to your own advantage.

7. *Calling All Women in Federal Service: Know Your Rights and Opportunities,* leaflet No. 53 of the Women's Bureau, United States Department of Labor, Employment Standards Administration, Women's Bureau, 1972. You can obtain a copy from the Superintendent of Documents, United States Government Printing Office, Washington, D.C. 20402, $.35.

In addition to all the information about how to put yourself into an executive job through foundation grants discussed in Section II, Chapter 4, you can learn more about obtaining grants from:

8. *Annual Register of Grant Support,* Academic Media, Orange, New Jersey. This is a comprehensive guide that can be obtained

at many good-sized libraries. It describes programs, conditions of eligibility, size of grants, and where to get applications and information for grants from government agencies, foundations, businesses, and professional organizations.

9. *Tips That Make Cents in Proposal Writing,* Women's Bureau, Employment Standards Administration, United States Department of Labor, Washington, D.C. 20210, free.

10. Below are three career-survey books containing hundreds of informative pages of listings and useful facts about standard jobs and professions:

How to Go to Work When Your Husband Is Against It, Your Children Aren't Old Enough, and There's Nothing You Can Do Anyhow, by Felice N. Schwartz, Margaret H. Schifter, and Susan S. Gillotti (New York: Simon & Schuster, Inc.,1972, $8.95; paperback, Simon & Schuster, Inc., 1975, $2.95).

New Job Opportunities for Women: Best Careers for Women Entering the Market for the First Time, Returning to Work, or Changing Positions by Muriel Lederer and the editors of *Consumer Guides* Publications International, Ltd. (Skokie, Ill.: *Consumer Guides* Publications International, Ltd. 1975; distributed by Simon & Schuster, Inc., New York, $8.95; paperback, New York: Quadrangle, 1976, $6.95).

No Experience Necessary: A Guide to Employment for the Female Liberal Arts Graduate by Sande Friedman and Lois C. Schwartz (New York: Dell Publishing Co., 1971, softcover, $1.25).

Apprenticeship Information

"Women in Apprenticeship, Why Not?" a three-year $105,000 United States research project concluded in 1974, discovered that the dropout rate for women apprentices is *half* that for men and that women receive a "high degree of employer satisfactions." Apprentice programs change constantly. Sometimes they are sponsored by labor unions carrying out United States Labor Department campaigns to train women (and minorities) in skilled trades. Sometimes they are outright federal efforts or local programs, which are occasionally union sponsored. According to the Labor Department, there are 415 apprenticeable occupations, about 160 of which already have women enrolled.

Places to Get Information About Apprenticeships

1. Your state department of labor; different states call this department by different names. If you cannot find it in your telephone book under the name of your state, ask any local politician. He or she will know.

2. Any of the ten regional offices of the Bureau of Apprenticeship Training of the United States Department of Labor. They are located in Boston, New York, Philadelphia, Atlanta, Chicago, Dallas, Kansas City, Missouri, Denver, San Francisco, and Seattle. Each office serves a group of surrounding states. Find it in the telephone book under "U.S. Government, Dept. of Labor."

3. Private groups with special programs (some of which are funded by government) to move women into apprenticeships:

Recruitment and Training Program, national headquarters at 162
       Fifth Avenue, New York, New York
Better Jobs for Women, Denver, Colorado
Advocates for Women, San Francisco, California
Milwaukee Women's Apprenticeship Aid Center, Milwaukee,
       Wisconsin
National Urban League, national headquarters at 500 E. 62nd
       Street, New York, New York

Arleen D. Winfield, a specialist with the Women's Bureau of the United States Department of Labor's Washington, D.C., office, emphasized during my interview with her that apprenticeships traditionally have been prized, lucrative plums because you earn while being taught a high-paying skill. As such, they have often been handed down within the trade to relatives and friends, a process that has effectively excluded not only male outsiders but also women and ethnic minorities. To counter this tradition, you may find the above agencies a help in making your way through the bureaucratic maze.

But while obtaining all the help you can from the agencies, do not discount the value of the direct approach. It, in the end, may open more doors than going through official channels. If you are personally acquainted with skilled trade union people, ask how you can become an apprentice for that group, and see what they and their personal contacts can accomplish for you. All the unions are under great federal pressure to seek out and accept women apprentices. If you have friends in the trade who can vouch for you, the unions may welcome you with open arms as the answer to their affirmative action problems.

4. Some useful publications:

Jobs for Which Apprenticeships Are Available, United States Department of Labor, Bureau of Labor Statistics, free. Leaflet explains qualifications and training required in the various trades and occupation outlook for them from now till 1985.

National Apprenticeship Program, United States Department of Labor, Manpower (sic) Administration, Washington, D.C. 20210; free. Provides a short explanation of the federal apprentice system together with a list of occupations and trades that use apprentices.

Steps to Opening the Skilled Trades to Women, Women's Bureau, Employment Standards Administration, United States Department of Labor, Washington, D.C. 20210, free.

The National Apprenticeship Program, United States Department of Labor, Manpower Administration, Bureau of Apprenticeship and Training, 32 pages, free. Explains the variety of agencies that can help you, apprenticeship laws and regulations.

Why Not Be an Apprentice? Leaflet No. 52 of the Women's Bureau, United States Department of Labor, Employment Standards Administration, Women's Bureau; reprinted 1974.

5
Succeeding Once You Have
Your Middle or Top Job

(Including more about Office Politics and how to make it work for you.)

Annually dozens of books dealing with the human relations aspects of job success pour from the nation's publishing houses. Below is a sampling of some good books. You will find others in your library. With rare exceptions, such as *The Peter Principle* or *Up the Organization,* business success books are not popularly distributed. Some publishers specialize in these kinds of books, and you can write to them and ask for their catalogues (free). Among them are the following:

> American Management Associations (also Amacom Imprint), 135 W. 50th Street, New York, New York 10020
> McGraw-Hill Book Company, General Business and Reference Department, 1221 Avenue of Americas, New York, New York 10020
> Prentice-Hall, Inc., Englewood Cliffs, New Jersey 07632

Some Good Books

1. *How to Get Control of Your Time and Your Life* by Alan Lakein, (New York: Peter H. Wyden, Inc., 1973, $6.95). Just what it says. The heart of the method and book in chapters 9 and 10 shows how to set priorities with Lakein's easily adopted A,B,C

lists. Absorbing and using his simple ideas (simple, after he tells them to you) can make the difference between enjoying your career plus family life and being torn apart by it.

2. *How to Read a Person Like a Book* by Gerald I. Nierenberg and Henry H. Calero, (Cornerstone Library 1971, paperback; distributed by Simon & Schuster, New York, $2.95). This book explains how to understand what people are really saying to you through body language. It is generously illustrated with drawings representing physical "words." Just as people's facial expressions mirror their feelings and reactions to what is happening, so do body gestures, movements, and postures. We all can and do learn to control our facial reactions and what we say, but almost no one is able to control his instinctive bodily reactions. The authors are a lawyer and a businessman, both of whom specialize in representing clients for high-power business negotiations. Their interpretations of what various gestures and stances mean have been proved out over the years, as they have learned to read these universal gestures in their opponents and take advantage of them.

3. *Bravely, Bravely in Business* by Richard R. Conarroe (New York: American Management Associations, Inc., 1972, $7.95). Here are thirty-two ground rules for personal success in your job— any job. Amusingly written, sprinkled with wry cartoons, this book nonetheless gives realistic, useful advice about how to understand and benefit from the motivations of people you work with and how to position yourself in the organization for maximum potential success and minimum vulnerability.

4. *The Executive Jungle: An Analysis of Personality Types Frequently Found in Executive Suites,* by Irwin L. Rodman (Los Angeles: Nash Publishing, 1972, $7.95). Written by an industrial psychologist and fun to read. The book takes you on a tour of such personalities as "The Manipulator," "The Man in the White Hat," "The Right Actor in the Wrong Play," and many more. It explains what makes them all tick and how to deal with them if you work with or for any of these types.

5. *How to Get Along with Almost Everybody* by Elton Reeves, (New York: Amacom, a division of American Management Associations, 1973, $8.75). If you supervise people, here is practical straightforward advice on working with "peers" and people both "up the line" and "down the line," There is also

information on customers, vendors, building a team, and other matters.

6. *The Ambitious Woman's Guide to a Successful Career* by Margaret V. Higginson and Thomas L. Quick (New York: Amacom, a division of American Management Associations, 1975, $9.95). This begins with the assumption that women have the ability and the right to succeed and proceeds from there. In matter-of-fact prose, the authors give practical advice to help the ambitious woman develop managerial skills and obtain and use job power.

7. *Bringing Women into Management,* edited by Francis E. Gordon and Myra H. Strober (New York: McGraw-Hill Book Company, Inc., 1975, $8.95). Plain discussion of basic strategies for bringing women into management, barriers that have kept women out, the law where it is and where it's going. The book gives vignettes of women in management, reviews major problems, suggests solutions.

8. *The Peter Principle* by Laurence J. Peter and Raymond Hull (New York: William Morrow & Company, Inc., 1969, $6.95, paperback $2.45). The classic. All about the people in business who have risen to their level of incompetence, this book helps explain a lot that goes on around you.

9. *Getting Through to People* by Jesse S. Nirenberg (Englewood Cliffs, N. J.: Prentice-Hall, Inc., 1963, softcover, $2.45; and *Breaking Through to Each Other: Creative Persuasion on the Job and in the Home,* by Jesse S. Nirenberg (New York: Harper & Row, Publishers, 1976, $7.95). Both of these books, written by an industrial psychologist, describe real situations with very practical, useful ideas about how to prevent verbal misunderstandings, how to persuade, and how to break through mental and emotional barriers. The author takes you through typical conversations remark by remark, showing how you go astray, how to make your words work. Interesting reading.

10. *Women's Work,* a bimonthly job / career magazine for women; 1649 K Street N.W., Washington, D.C. 20006; $5.00 for six issues. Attractive format. It tells you how to get a job, succeed at it, change your job, get a promotion and so on.

11. *The Executive Woman,* a monthly newsletter for the woman with her own business or for the woman who is moving up the

executive ladder; 747 Third Avenue, New York, New York 10017; 6 pages, $20.00 a year. News, interviews, and encouragement.

The above two publications are a supplement to the mainstream literature. They may give you some insights that can help you meet and best antiwoman business prejudices or barriers. They are definitely not a substitute for keeping yourself informed through the basic business publications that your male peers will be reading and that are just as important for you: *The Wall Street Journal, Fortune, Business Week,* and many others.

12. *A Working Woman's Guide to Job Rights,* Leaflet No. 55, United States Department of Labor, Employment Standards Administration, Women's Bureau, revised 1975. Obtain this from the Superintendent of Documents, United States Government Printing Office, Washington, D.C. 20402, $.65. Readable, useful 34-page pamphlet, telling in plain language what you need to know about maternity leaves, discrimination in promotion, equal pay, minimum wages, overtime pay, social security benefits, tax deductions for child care and household help and more.

13. *Everything a Woman Needs to Know to Get Paid What She's Worth* by Caroline Bird (New York: David McKay, Inc., 1973, $8.95; paperback, Bantam, $1.95). A question-and-answer format that seems to cover all everything you might want to know.

14. *Getting Yours* by Letty Cottin Pogrebin (New York: David McKay, Inc., 1975, $8.95; paperback, Avon, $1.75). How to get a job, how to make the law work for you, and how to cope simultaneously with career and family.

15. *Male Chauvinism: How It Works,* by Michael Korda (New York: Random House, Inc., 1972, $6.95). Useful as an eye-opener.

16. *The Mother Who Works Outside the Home* by Sally Wendkos Olds (New York: The Child Study Association of America, 1975, softcover, $1.50). Middle-of-the-road, intelligent advice not only on how to cope with career and family simultaneously but also on how to help the whole family enjoy it.

6
Getting College Credits
in Offbeat Ways

1. College Level Examination Program (C.L.E.P.), Educational Testing Service, Princeton, New Jersey. In Section I, Chapter 4, we discussed this program, through which you can take examinations to receive college credit for self-taught, life-learned knowledge. C.L.E.P. does not itself award you the college credit. You obtain the credit by taking the C.L.E.P. examinations that are given at over 300 colleges in a wide variety of subjects. Most colleges will then grant you college credit based on your passing the examination in a particular subject. Write to C.L.E.P. for full particulars and subjects involved.

2. College Proficiency Examinations Program (C.P.E.P.). Given by the New York State Education Department, they are useful to you no matter where you live in the United States. New York State offers *external* college degrees to anyone in the United States who can meet requirements through courses at an accredited institution and/or C.L.E.P. and C.P.E.P. Write to Regents External Degrees, New York State Education Department, Room 1924, 99 Washington Avenue, Albany, New York 12210.

3. *University Without Walls: A First Report,*1972. This booklet explains the University Without Walls program, which allows you to obtain a college degree through home study materials, and lists participating institutions. Write to Dr. Samuel Baskin, Union for Experimenting Colleges and Universities, Antioch College, Yellow Springs, Ohio 45307.

4. Women's Equity Action League (W.E.A.L.), Educational

and Legal Defense Fund, National Press Building, Washington, D.C. 20045. Publishes a very useful, large, 35-page booklet on women and college fellowships and how to get them; $4.00 first-class mail, $3.50 third class. The W.E.A.L. booklet suggests some other useful sources: *A Selected List of Major Fellowship Opportunities and Aids to Advanced Education for United States Citizens,* National Academy of Sciences, Washington, D.C. This is available from the National Research Council, Commission on Human Resources, 2101 Constitution Avenue N.W., Washington, D.C. 20418. *A Selected List of Professional Training Programs and Interneships,* American Association of University Women, 2401 Virginia Avenue N.W., Washington, D.C. 20037. *Scholarships, Fellowships, and Loans* by Norman Feingold, (Cambridge, Mass.: 02138 Bellman Publishing Co., 1972). *Awards for Graduate Study and Research,* Dominion Bureau of Statistics, Education Dvision, Ottawa 3, Ontario, Canada.

5. *Women's Stake in Low Tuition,* American Association of State Colleges and Universities, Suite 700, 1 Dupont Circle, Washington, D.C. 20036, free. Sensible, useful 16-page pamphlet explaining why you as a woman and a voter should support low tuitions at public local and state colleges.

6. *The Value of College: A Noneconomist's View,* Ford Foundation; Office of Reports, 320 E. 43rd Street, New York, New York 10017, 1975, 1976, free. Small brochure reprint of a speech by Harold Howe II, vice-president, Division of Education and Research of the Ford Foundation, putting forth the cultural and personal advantages of a college education.

7. *Get Credit for What You Know,* leaflet No. 56 of the Women's Bureau, United States Department of Labor, Employment Standards Administration, Women's Bureau, 1974, $.30. Obtain from the Superintendent of Documents, United States Government Printing Office, Washington, D.C. 20402.

7
How to Go into Business for Yourself

1. Section VIII, Chapter 2, discusses many publications and kinds of help you can obtain from your area Small Business Administration office. Many of the publications and the counseling are free. United States (SBA) offices are located in the following cities:

SBA Field Offices

Agana, GU	Cincinnati, OH
Albany, NY	Clarksburg, WV
Albuquerque, NM	Cleveland, OH
Anchorage, AK	Columbia, SC
Atlanta, GA	Columbus, OH
Augusta, ME	Concord, NH
Baltimore, MD	Coral Gables, FL
Biloxi, MS	Corpus Christi, TX
Birmingham, AL	Dallas, TX
Boise, ID	Denver, CO
Boston, MA	Des Moines, IA
Buffalo, NY	Detroit, MI
Camden, NJ	Eau Claire, WI
Casper, WY	Elmira, NY
Charleston, WV	El Paso, TX
Charlotte, NC	Fairbanks, AK
Chicago, IL	Fargo, ND

Fresno, CA
Greenville, NC
Harrisburg, PA
Hartford, CT
Hato Rey, PR
Helena, MT
Holyoke, MA
Honolulu, HI
Houston, TX
Indianapolis, IN
Jackson, MS
Jacksonville, FL
Jericho, NY
Kansas City, MO
Knoxville, TN
Las Vegas, NE
Little Rock, AR
Los Angeles, CA
Louisville, KY
Lower Rio Grande
   Valley, TX
Lubbock, TX
Madison, WI
Marquette, MI
Marshall, TX
Memphis, TN
Milwaukee, WI
Minneapolis, MN
Montpelier, VT
Nashville, TN
Newark, NJ
New Orleans, LA

New York, NY
Oklahoma City, OK
Omaha, NE
Philadelphia, PA
Phoenix, AZ
Pittsburgh, PA
Portland, OR
Providence, RI
Rapid City, SD
Reno, NE
Richmond, VA
Rochester, NY
St. Louis, MO
Sacramento, CA
Salt Lake City, UT
San Antonio, TX
San Diego, CA
San Francisco, CA
Seattle, WA
Shreveport, LA
Sioux Falls, SD
Spokane, WA
Springfield, IL
St. Thomas, VI
Syracuse, NY
Tampa, FL
Washington, DC
West Palm Beach, FL
Wichita, KS
Wilkes-Barre, PA
Wilmington, DE

2. Bank of America offers a series of very useful aids and publications: *Small Business Reporter,* published 10 times annually, is available free at any Bank of America community office, or may be ordered by mail, at $1.00 per copy, through Department 3120, Bank of America, P. O. Box 37000, San Francisco, California 94137. The publication offers thorough

research, including extensive field interviewing, dealing with the investment required, operational format, and hazards and opportunities of specific businesses. It also explains various aspects of business management and operations related to problems business people encounter in all fields. Emphasis is placed on California-based operations, *but the material is applicable throughout the United States.*

Bank of America also offers a very useful series of softcover books dubbed "Business Profile." Each deals with a specific industry: for example, home furnishing stores, gift stores, plant stores, apparel stores, sewing and needlecraft centers, small-job printing, proprietary day care. The books are $1.00 apiece at the *Small Business Reporter* address. These profiles guide you through rental agreements, store design, exterior and interior floor plan, lighting, store fixtures, financing, trade shows, buying centers, buying terms and discounts, minimums and exclusives, inventory control, pricing, security, personnel, and so on. For a complete list of Bank of America self-help publications for business people, ask for their Publication Index (free) from the *Small Business Reporter* address.

3. *How to Get Big Results from a Small Advertising Budget* by Cynthia S. Smith, (New York: Hawthorn Books, Inc., 1973, $7.95). Do-it-yourself market research, media selection, copywriting, direct mail, public relations, visual sales presentations, secrets of a successful catalogue, point-of-purchase displays, and more, are all discussed in easy-reading, anecdotal style.

4. *Supergirls* by Claudia Jessup and Genie Chipps(New York: Harper & Row, Publishers, 1972). How, with brains, energy, and imagination, two young women set up their own business and had fun doing it. Delightful reading with a lot of sensible advice woven in. You can profit from the authors' mistakes and adopt their breakthrough ideas.

5. *Organizations that can help you*

Sweeping generalizations are dangerous. So we will not say "every" but we will say for "almost every" business that you can start, there is a national organization of owners of similar businesses. These organizations can supply you with all kinds of specialized, useful information that helps you make your business profitable. Ask your suppliers. They will probably know which is "your" organization. Or, check the following books in your library:

> *National Trade and Professional Associations of the United States*, Columbia Books, Inc., 734 15th Street N.W., Washington, D.C. 20005.

> *Encyclopedia of Associations and National Organizations of the United States*, Volume I, Gale Research Company, Book Tower, Detroit, Michigan 48226.

6. *Publications that can help you*

Again, "almost every" kind of business that you can think of is served by at least one (and frequently by two, three, or four) publications. For example, are you thinking of opening some kind of specialty home furnishings store? Take your choice from those below; and there are lots more we are not listing.

> *China Glass and Tablewares*, 1115 Clifton Avenue, Clifton, New Jersey 07013, monthly. Publishes articles for specialty shop and department store merchants; describes merchandising ideas, special promotion, display techniques, advertising programs, and retail activities in this field.

All the following cover their businesses with the same practical concentration on techniques to help you display, advertise, sell, and make a profit. They usually are monthlies, occasionally bimonthly or weekly.

> *Furniture & Furnishings*, 1450 Don Mills Road, Don Mills, Ontario, Canada

> *Linens, Domestics, and Bath Products*, 370 Lexington Avenue, New York, New York 10017

> *Gifts and Decorative Accessories*, 51 Madison Avenue, New York, New York 10010

> *Flooring Magazine*, 757 Third Avenue, New York 10017

> *Upholstering Industry Magazine*, 600 S. Michigan Avenue

Chicago, Illinois 60605. for "upholstery manufacturers, custom upholsterers, furniture designers, fabric distributors"

Gift and Tableware Reporter, 1515 Broadway, New York, New York 10036

Maybe you have office equipment and office supplies in mind:

Office World News, 645 Stewart Avenue, Garden City, New York 11530

Southern Stationer and Office Outfitter, 75 Third Street N.W., Atlanta, Georgia 30308. "For retailers of office products in the Southeast and Southwest ... contents deal with solving problems of store layout, inventory, personnel, etc."

Office Products, Hitchcock Building, Wheaton, Illinois 60187. "Established in 1904 for independent dealers who sell all types of office products—machines, furniture, office supplies...."

Perhaps you hope to set up a campground:

Campground and RV Park Management, P.O. Box 1014, Grass Valley, California 95945

Park Maintenance, P.O. Box 409, Appleton, Wisconsin

Or is your interest covered by one of the following, among other miscellaneous journals?

Health Foods Business, 225 W. 34th Street, New York, New York 10001

American Firearms Industry, 70001 N. Clark Street, Chicago, Ill. 60625. "For retailers of firearms and accessories."

Army/Navy Store and Outdoor Merchandiser, 225 W. 34th Street, New York, New York 10001

College Store Executive, 211 Broadway, Lynbrook, New York

11563. "For managers, buyers, and business operators of campus stores."

Specialty Bakers Voice, 299 Broadway, New York, New York 10007. "Geared to the single unit and multi-unit retail bake shop."

Well, you get the idea. If you do not know which journals serve your kind of business, ask some of your suppliers. Do not stop asking when you receive one name. There are probably two or more publications specifically aimed at your kind of business. Or consult the *Ayer Directory of Publications* in its Trade, Technical, and Class Section. This directory is one of those books that almost every library has. Published by Ayer Press Publishing Division of N. W. Ayer, A.B.H. International, Philadelphia. Another directory, simpler to use, which your library might have, is *The Standard Periodical Directory*, Oxbridge Publishing Company, New York.

7. *Artemis*, newsletter for women business owners, monthly, 8 pages $14 annually, 250 W. 57th Street New York, New York 10019. Interviews with women who have created various kinds of businesses and tell how they did it; some general business information for all business owners.

8
Overview of Other Women's
Get-a-Job Books,
Articles, Programs

This book represents a new viewpoint. To see how it differs from
what has gone before, let us skim what has previously been
researched and discussed.

Sometimes when an idea finally arrives, it is so correct for the
age that we lose our perspective of time and begin to think the
idea hoary. It was only in 1963 and 1964 when Betty Friedan was
touring the nation painstakingly explaining "the feminine mystique" to skeptical print, radio, and TV interviewers. For the rest
of the decade, conversations, demonstrations, and writings on the
subject were occupied with arguing the validity of Friedan's
thesis. It was 1966 before the National Organization of Women
(N.O.W.) was formed and 1968, 1969, and 1970 before the
interest of the women's movement's in careers had even a light
impact on the country.

As late as 1970, women interviewed in a major nationwide poll
by Louis Harris and Associates declared themselves 42 percent
against wanting to change women's status in society to 40 percent
supporting changes (18 percent not sure). Only a tiny 11 percent
believed "women wanting better jobs, better pay, equal pay with
men" were worthy of support. As for job conditions, what was
there to fuss about anyhow? The women in the 1970 poll—not just
women, but the working women portion of the group—still at that
late date agreed *by sizable margins* that women were already
being given an equal chance on the job.

Isolated researchers were producing other evidence. Matina
Horner's famed "fear of success" study dates from 1968. (An

interesting failure to replicate, which led to questioning of Horner's methodology and possibly her results, was published in the January 1975 *American Journal of Sociology).* Margaret Hennig's research into the characteristics and background of successful women executives was completed in 1971. However, so little did the research on women and work of that period penetrate the national consciousness, that on January 14, 1973, *The New York Times Magazine,* which insists on a fresh news peg for all its articles, could run a major piece reporting Horner's study as if it were new information.

During the transition years from 1968 to 1973, as women and men had previously debated the "morality" and accuracy of Betty Friedan's thesis, so, then, research and writings concentrated on documenting, proving, and discussing women's overall second-class status, including their second-class job status. For job status there were mass appeal books like Caroline Bird's *Born Female: The High Cost of Keeping Women Down* (New York: David McKay, Company, Inc., 1968), which produced much debate; also scholarly books like Cynthia Fuchs Epstein's *Women's Place: Options and Limits in Professional Careers,* (Berkeley and Los Angeles: University of California Press, 1970); as well as excellent collections of writings that analyzed social, personal, familial, and educational factors affecting women's career aspirations and performance. *Women & Success: The Anatomy of Achievement,* edited by Ruth B. Kundsin (New York: The New York Academy of Sciences and William Morrow & Company, Inc., 1973, 1974) is an excellent book of this type. Another collection that has become a classic, *Women in Sexist Society: Studies in Power and Powerlessness,* edited by Vivian Gornick and Barbara K. Moran (New York: Basic Books, 1971), brought together some of the best feminist writers to discuss various noncareer feminist issues and included six valuable chapters again documenting and explaining how and why the work world functions to exclude women.

Of course, these were also the years of books on women's lives and roles in general: *The Female Eunuch, Sexual Politics, Women and Madness,* and others.

When, in March 1972, the Equal Employment Opportunity Commission (EEOC) received enforcement powers, it soon stunned the business world (in January 1973) by winning its $50 million damage suit against A.T.&T. The corporation *admitted in writing* that they habitually prevented women from rising to significant supervisory or executive rank. Public interest followed in the wake of the feminists' battle; there was an upsurge in research and publications on how a woman could make affirmative action laws work for her, and how she could cope simultaneously with children, husband, and career once she did find a job. The government fanned public interest by quickly filing 150 other cases against such giants as Mobil Oil, American Tobacco, Metropolitan Life, General Electric, the Container Corporation of America, Standard Brands, General Motors Corporation, and Chrysler Corporation.

During these years, Catalyst, the women's organization, developed its part-time job concept of "one job, two women" and offered it, together with a distillation of the past few years' developments (a discussion of why you and your family will be happier if you add a job to your life, advice on how to cope, and a career Baedeker) in its book, *How to Go to Work When Your Husband Is Against It, Your Children Aren't Old Enough, And There's Nothing You Can Do Anyhow* (New York: Simon & Schuster, Inc., 1972). It was accompanied and followed by other good mass-appeal books in this vein, and these have continued to appear to this day, as have scholarly treatments of the subjects such as *The Two Career Family* by Lynda Lytle Holmstrom (Cambridge, Mass.: Schenkman Publishing Company, 1973).

Simultaneously, from the beginning of the movement to the present, sociologists and psychologists have examined various aspects of the women-and-jobs topic. They have conducted investigations according to their own interests and have reported their findings at professional conventions and in important research journals like *Journal of Marriage and the Family, Journal of Applied Psychology, Journal of Personality,* and *Journal of Psychology.* Studies range from such intriguing-sounding ones as "Assertiveness and Sexual Satisfaction in Employed Professional Women" and "Success Orientation and Sex-Role Congruence as Determinants of the Attractiveness of Competent Women" to "Influence of Sex-Role Stereotypes on Evaluation of Male and Female Supervisory Behavior," "Professional Women's Tolerance of Domestication," and many others.

Elsewhere, other research has dealt with women and careers from the point of view of people's feelings on the subject. We have mentioned the 1970 Louis Harris Poll. A 1972 effort, the joint Institute for Social Research–*Redbook* Magazine survey was probably the largest serious poll ever attempted: 120,000 women. In the new landmark massive report, *The Quality of American Life: Perceptions, Evaluations, and Satisfactions* (New York: Russell Sage Foundation, 1976), Angus Campbell, Philip Converse, and Willard Rodgers of the University of Michigan's Institute for Social Research have also examined how people feel about many things, including women's jobs.

In the business literature, there have been excellent guides published to help women succeed through standard career channels. Some, like *Breakthrough: Women into Management* by Rosalind Loring and Theodora Wells (New York: Van Nostrand Reinhold Company, 1972) and *The Ambitious Woman's Guide to a Successful Career* (New York: Amacom, American Management Associations, 1975), are leavened with psychological and sociological insights into pertinent problems.

Serious business periodicals have investigated and reported other aspects of the issues; for example, *M.B.A.* magazine devoted an issue to executive women, penetratingly exposing the difference between corporate utterances of interest in women and the actual hiring of them, and *Harvard Business Review* published an article on "Sex Stereotyping in the Executive Suite." Other important business service publications like *Management Review, Personnel, S.A.M. Advanced Management Journal,* and *Personnel Administration/Public Personnel Review,* have given Catalyst's president, Felice N. Schwartz, space to put forth the organization's ideas or have featured articles from time to time discussing methods and problems associated with bringing women into middle- and upper-level jobs. The mass-circulation prestigious business publications, like *Fortune* and *Business Week,* have contented themselves with running occasional articles on the "Ten Highest Ranking Women in Business" or "The Top 100 Corporate Women" and spinoffs of this theme.

The United States Labor Department researchers and individual researchers, including some supported by grants from various of the private foundations, have undertaken different kinds of projects. They have documented the conditions of women at work (status of and future prospects of working-class women, efforts to improve the status of household workers, and so on) and have compiled valuable statistics of all kinds.

Overall, the private foundations' efforts have been minimal. In the spring of 1975 the president of N.O.W.'s Legal Defense and Education Fund castigated them for failing to support research into women's problems. She pointed out that since 1972 less than *one-fifth of one percent of foundation grant money* has been funneled into programs designed to improve women's status.

In summary, then, this book's viewpoint—straight to the middle or the top and how to do it—is a new approach to women and work that has not yet been investigated or discussed in books, university research, magazine articles, women's groups, United States government studies, or foundation programs.

Notes And Sources

Preface

John O'Riley, "The Outlook, Review of Current Trends in Business and Finance," *The Wall Street Journal,* March 8, 1976, p. 1.

Women's Bureau,"Women Workers Today," United States Department of Labor, Employment Standards Administration, July 1975, pp. 2–7, revised.

Work in America Institute, Inc., *World of Work Report,* Vol. 1, No. 10 (December 1976), p. 1.

YOUR VOLUNTEER EXPERIENCES CAN START YOU IN THE MIDDLE OR AT THE TOP

Columbia University Press, which distributes *The Foundation Directory* mentioned in this section, is located at 562 W. 113th Street, New York, New York 10025.

Vanguard Press, publisher of *The Art of Winning Foundation Grants,* is located at 424 Madison Avenue, New York, New York 10017.

Plenum Press, publisher of *Grants: How to Find Out About Them and What to Do Next?,* is located at 227 W. 17th Street, New York, New York 10011.

Information about grant aid to constituents is from my interview with New Jersey Senator Harrison Williams's grant specialist, Wallace Johnson.

Janice LaRouche and Mary Scott Welch, "Women on the Job" column, *McCall's,* April 1975, pp. 68, 70.

Dr. Henry W. Wriston, "It's All in Your Mind," *The New York Times,* June 11, 1975, Op-Ed page.

EXPERIENCE HELPING YOUR HUSBAND WITH HIS JOB OR BUSINESS CAN START YOU IN THE MIDDLE OR AT THE TOP

Business Economics Department, Dun & Bradstreet, Inc., *The Business Failure Record 1973*, Dun & Bradstreet, Inc., New York, August 1974, p. 3.

Comments of Dorothy Becker, corporate vice-president, Staff Builders, are from my interview with her.

Administrative Management Society, eds., *Office Salaries: Directory for United States and Canada*, the 28th annual survey, 1975–1976. The address of the society is Maryland Road, Willow Grove, Pennsylvania 19090.

Judy Klemesrud "She Shrugs If They Slam a Door on Her," *The New York Times*, July 8, 1971.

GREAT TWO- TO SIX-HOUR-A-WEEK JOBS

Comments of Charles Wood, executive director of the Adult Education Association of the United States of America, Washington, D.C., are from a telephone interview with me. The A.E.A. is at 810 18th Street, N.W., Washington, D.C.

Another organization that provides support and information for community schools is the National Community School Education Association (N.C.S.E.A.), which publishes the N.C.S.E.A NEWS, 1017 Avon Street Flint, Michigan 48503. This organization has ties with local college and community groups. Obtain addresses for groups near you from their Michigan headquarters.

Marvin E. Shaw and Stephen T. Margulis, "The Power of the Printed Word," *Journal of Social Psychology*, (December 1974): 301–302.

LAUNCHING A CAREER IN POLITICS

Jeane J. Kirkpatrick, *Political Woman* (New York: Basic Books, 1974), p. 45.

The "who's who of women in public office" referred to in the text is *Women in Public Office: A Biographical Directory and Statistical Analysis*, compiled by the Center for American Women and Politics C.A.W.P.), published in 1976. Available from R. R. Bowker Order Department, P.O. Box 1807, Ann Arbor, Michigan 48106, $19.95. "Women in Elected Office: Some Bad News and Some Good" is a three-page news release based on the above compilation of *Women in Public Office*. The release offers some of the statistical highlights found in the complete directory and statistical analysis. The release can be obtained free from C.A.W.P., The Eagleton Institute of Politics, Wood Lawn, Neilson Campus, New Brunswick, New Jersey, 08901.

Quotes by Barbara Mikulski and Ann Lewis are from Eileen Shanahan, "Women Are Found to Hold 5% of Elected Office," *The New York Times*, January 26, 1976, p. 1.

Susan Tolchin and Martin Tolchin, *Clout, Womanpower, and Politics* (New York: Coward, McCann & Geoghegan, 1973.), p. 234 of paperback Capricorn edition.

Louis Harris and Associates, "A Survey of the Attitudes of Women on Their Roles in Politics and the Economy," *The 1972 Virginia Slims American Women's Opinion Poll Monograph*, 1972, pp. 35–38.

Comment of Dr. Ruth B. Mandel, director, C.A.W.P., is from a telephone interview with me.

Anita Siegenthaler's comments are from Peter Golenbock, "Women's Slant Expanding on Public Affairs," *The Record*, Hackensack, New Jersey, January 3, 1976.

Interview with Mrs. Linda Winikow is from Roberta Roesch, "What Do You Want to Do?" column, *The Record*, Hackensack, New Jersey, March 30, 1975.

Marilyn Johnson and Kathy Stanwick, *Profile of Women Holding Office*. This is a 36-page summary of *Women in Public Office: A Biographical Directory and Statistical Analysis*. The summary is available from C.A.W.P., Eagleton Institute, Wood Lawn, Neilson Campus, New Brunswick, New Jersey 08901, $3.00.

HIGH-PAYING JOBS AND CAREERS BY AVOIDING THE STANDARD "WOMEN'S JOBS"

June Bingham, "Small Skirmish with Racism," *Harper's Weekly*, January 12, 1976, p. 7.

Janice Neipert Hedges, "Women Workers and Manpower Demands in the 1970s," *Monthly Labor Review*, United States Department of Labor, Bureau of Labor Statistics, 19,23,24.

Personnel Journal, May 1975, p. 257.

The Record, Hackensack, New Jersey, February 25, 1975.

Jon J. Durkin, "The Potential of Women," Johnson O'Connor Research Foundation Human Engineering Laboratory Bulletin No. 87. The address of the foundation is 347 Beacon Street, Boston, Massachusetts 02116.

The Record, Hackensack, New Jersey, October 17, 1972.

Interview with George Wyatt, director, New York City office, Johnson O'Connor Research Foundation.

Quote from American Dental Association is from *Newark Sunday Star Ledger*, March 12, 1972.

Physicians' statistics are from Hedges, "Women Workers," p. 24.

The facts concerning Sandra Gourley are from Lisa Hammel, *The New York Times*, December 14, 1971, p. 58.

The comments on income are from Michael Jett, *The Wall Street Journal*, April 16, 1973.

Betsy Medsger, *Women at Work*, (New York: Sheed and Ward, Inc., 1975); also interview of Medsger by Judy Klemesrud, *The New York Times*, August 13, 1975.

Quotes from Janet Jones, Juliette Moran, and Gertrude McWilliams are from Milton Rockmore, "View from the Top," syndicated newspaper column for week of May 2, 1976.

EVEN NONEXISTENT OR RUSTY SKILLS CAN MEAN A MIDDLE- OR TOP-LEVEL JOB

Robert J. Jameson, *The Professional Job Changing System*, Performance Dynamics, 17 Grove Avenue, Verona, New Jersey, 07044, 1974, pp. 24, 164.

Eli Djeddah, *Moving Up*, (Philadelphia: J. B. Lippincott Company, 1970), pp. 88, 89–104.

Western Temporary information may be obtained through their New York City national agent, Lobsenz-Stevens, Inc., 645 Madison Avenue, New York, New York 10022.

Ury (sic) M. Gluskinos and Bruce J. Kestelman, "Management and Labor Leaders' Perception of Worker Needs as Compared with Self-Reported Needs," *Personnel Psychology: A Journal of Applied Research*. If you wish to send for a copy, the address of the journal is 3121 Cheek Road, Durham, North Carolina 27704. Summer 1971 issue.

Esmark, Inc., 55 East Monroe Street, Chicago, Illinois 60603.

Alison Goddard, "Mature Woman Counsels Others Returning to College," Information Center on the Mature Woman, January 1975; 515 Madison Avenue, New York, New York 10022.

For George Washington University grades, see David M. Elsner, "More Older Women Return to College; Most Do Very Well," *The Wall Street Journal*, September 12, 1972, p. 1.

"Student Reactions to College," Educational Testing Service, Princeton, New Jersey, 1972, 1974.

YOUR "IMPOSSIBLE DREAM": A BUSINESS OF YOUR OWN

Dr. Witkin's comments are from my interview with him.

Madeline McWhinney's comments are taken from Marylin Bender, "More Women Becoming Owners of Businesses." *The New York Times,* April 25, 1976, p. 1.

Edwin E. Ghiselli, "Some Motivational Factors in the Success of Managers," Table No. 1, "Items Significantly Differentiating Those for Whom Job Security Is Important from Those for Whom It Is Not (Winter 1968): 434.

Catherine C. Arnott, "Husbands' Attitude and Wives' Commitment to Employment," *Journal of Marriage and the Family,* (November 1972): 673–684.